# KEY TO SYMBOLS

**Leaf s** ... **tion in Europe**

**Evergr**

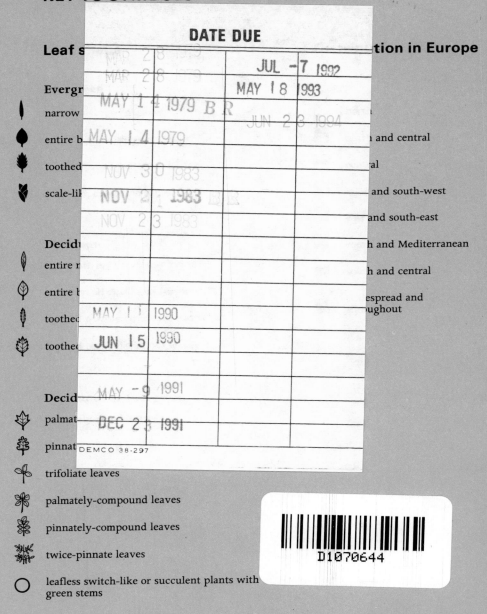

| narrow | |
| entire b | and central |
| toothed | al |
| scale-lik | and south-west |
| | and south-east |

**Decidu** ... h and Mediterranean

| entire r | h and central |
| entire b | espread and |
| toothed | ughout |
| toothed | |

**Decid**

| palmat | |
| pinnat | |

trifoliate leaves

palmately-compound leaves

pinnately-compound leaves

twice-pinnate leaves

leafless switch-like or succulent plants with green stems

| cm | 0 | 1 | 2 | 3 | 4 | 5 | 6 | 7 | 8 | 9 | 10 | 11 |
| mm | 0 5 | 10 | 20 | 30 | 40 | 50 | 60 | 70 | 80 | 90 | 100 | 110 |

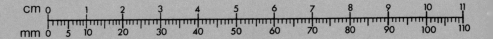

# Trees and Bushes of Europe

# Trees and Bushes of Europe

OLEG POLUNIN
with drawings by
BARBARA EVERARD

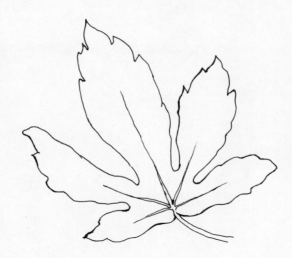

LONDON

## Oxford University Press

NEW YORK · TORONTO

1976

*Oxford University Press, Ely House, London W.1*

LONDON OXFORD GLASGOW NEW YORK
TORONTO MELBOURNE WELLINGTON
CAPE TOWN IBADAN NAIROBI DAR ES SALAAM LUSAKA ADDIS ABABA
KUALA LUMPUR SINGAPORE JAKARTA HONG KONG TOKYO
DELHI BOMBAY CALCUTTA MADRAS KARACHI

ISBN 0 19 217631 5

Filmset in Great Britain by
BAS Printers, Wallop, Hampshire
Colour Origination and printing Heraclio Fournier, S.A.
VITORIA - SPAIN

# Contents

‡ in text indicates a species introduced from outside Europe.

† in text indicates that the species is illustrated in the *Barks* section.

* in text indicates that the species is included in the *Uses* appendix.

All illustrations are of the species in the bold heading of the entry alongside them unless otherwise stated.

The botanical drawings are reproduced half life size unless otherwise stated.

# Preface

This book will enable the user to identify all the native trees and bushes that grow wild in Europe to over two metres—above a man's height. (The distinction between a tree and a bush is not a scientific one, but on the whole a tree has a single trunk, while a bush has several woody stems arising from close to the ground.) The book also includes alien trees and bushes which have been introduced to Europe and are now grown in forests or orchards, or are frequently planted as roadside or boulevard trees, as well as naturalized species that can propagate themselves and hold their own in native vegetation; but excludes those usually seen only in parks and gardens. Introduced species are marked ‡ in the text.

The precise criterion for inclusion or exclusion of introduced or naturalized species is difficult to fix. *Flora Europaea*, the standard work, has been closely followed and almost all species described in it that qualify in stature are included here. The only exceptions are in certain genera containing a number of very similar-looking species, when only the most commonly encountered and most distinctive species are described. Thus some minutely differing species of oaks, whitebeams, pears, hawthorns, and tamarisks have been rejected. A few additional species that the author has noted on his own travels have been included.

The selection of two metres as the qualifying height is less arbitrary than it may seem, coinciding in many genera with a 'natural' demarcation between the lower bushes and the distinctly taller species able to overshadow all herbaceous and many woody plants. In a few cases the dividing line is indeed arbitrary as, for example, in the heathers. Here only four species out of a total of sixteen often grow above two metres under normal field conditions. Some species grow to over two metres only in favourable environments, these have generally been included; others may reach this height only in cultivation, these are usually excluded. In general the heights of species given are those recorded in *Flora Europaea*. The inclusion of smaller shrubs, sub-shrubs and shrublets would have greatly increased the number of species, and defeated the aims of producing a readily portable book. Europe, as defined by *Flora Europaea*, differs somewhat from common practice, and for obvious reasons the Azores and Russia east of latitude 30° (a line drawn roughly through Leningrad and Kiev), the Crimea, and the Caucasus are not embraced in this book. Turkey-in-Europe, and the Eastern Aegean islands, including Rhodes, are included.

The arrangement of families is in accordance with the 'natural order' as accepted by most European botanists. Brief descriptions are given of the main families, and their salient features illustrated. Where there are several important genera in a family (as, for example, the Rose Family, which covers hawthorns, apples, prunuses, pears, etc.), illustrated keys guide one to the right genus; where a genus has a large number of European species (as, for example, pears which include Wild Pear, Common Pear, Almond-Leaved Pear, etc.) further keys help the reader track down the individual tree he is looking at. The working of these keys is explained on p. vii.

The illustrations are designed to show as many different characters of the tree as possible. While the colour in the photographs is accurate, it must not be taken too literally: the colour of a leaf varies according as to whether it is from the top or bottom branches of the same tree, and with age, the soil, the climatic conditions, and so on. Seven pages are devoted to photographs of different barks for the sake of comparison; trees included in this section are indicated † in the text. The drawings and paintings are half life-size unless otherwise specified.

An appendix provides additional fascinating information on the uses to man of many species described; these are marked * in the text.

## To use this book

Unquestionably for most people careful and repeated study of the photographs and paintings will be the quickest way of getting to know the species by name. But should you find a species you do not recognize, the symbols indicating its leaf shape—and additionally where it is to be found in Europe—will help in tracking it down. (The identification of leafless winter trees and bushes presents a problem. Some are distinctive and are soon mastered, but others are very similar in appearance and can only be learned after considerable effort and experience. No simple key can be devised to pin down the subtle variations in bark, buds, lenticels, and hairs.) Having established the leaf shape of your plant (see p. viii), you can look it up in the Leaf Check List (p. xiii). This will lead you to one of several groups of species or genera; then by a process of elimination, carefully checking your specimen point by point with the text, photographs, paintings, and drawings, you can make your identification.

For the larger genera there are the typical dichotomous keys to aid you. They pose contrasting pairs of questions, one of which should fit your specimen and be answered in the affirmative (provided you are studying the correct genus). This will lead you to the next pair of questions, numbered consecutively with the first, and again you should be able to answer 'yes' to one of the alternatives, thus giving you the name of the plant, or leading you on to the next pair of questions, and so on. Having found the answer by means of the key, carefully check your specimen for as many details as possible against the description and illustrations.

Some of the keys of the most difficult genera are not easy to work. Lack of familiarity with the terms and ideas used in the key, or the fact that flowers or fruits are not available at the time, may make an exact identification difficult; considerable experience of genera such as *Crataegus, Sorbus, Quercus,* and *Pinus* is required before correct diagnosis can be assured. You must study your plants at different seasons of the year and try to look at a number of samples rather than base your judgement on an individual specimen; and remember too that hybrids with intermediate characters to the parent species, or local variants may not 'fit the key'.

Care must also be taken in using the leaf-shape and distribution symbols. It must be insisted that in each case the symbols can only be 'indicators', and can not be interpreted too rigidly. A number of species could with justification be placed in more than one category. Some may think of gorse, for example, as having no leaves, while others might think of its spines as needles. In the text it can be allocated only one symbol (though the Leaf Check List, which includes it under both, should put you on the right track). Should you be looking at leaves from the sucker shoot of the Aspen rather than at leaves from the main branches, again you will arrive at a wrong conclusion. Be sure, too, that you understand the differences between the symbols—for example the difference between the simple leaves of the Box and the pinnately compound leaves of the False Acacia, or between deciduous and evergreen leaves. While the former are shed in autumn, the latter remain on the twigs over the winter and usually for more than one year. Old leaves of previous years can generally be distinguished not only by their colour and texture, but by the fact that they arise on older twigs, usually themselves differently coloured from the terminal present year's twigs. Second-year twigs have thicker and darker bark, and sometimes rings of bud scars can be seen to separate the wood of different years. The last seven leaf shapes listed below can be either deciduous or evergreen, though the majority are deciduous. Plants appearing under these symbols are deciduous unless it is otherwise stated in the text.

The symbols, listed for convenience on the inside of the cover, can be explained as follows:

**NARROW EVERGREEN LEAVES**—more than twice as long as broad. Often needle-like and less than 5 mm wide; rounded, quadrangular, or triangular in section; often flattened, with a distinct upper and lower surface. Apex sharp-pointed, acute, blunt, or notched. Alternatively more than 5 mm wide, varying from broadly lanceolate, oblanceolate, oblong to linear; always flattened with distinct upper and lower surface. Leaf margin usually not toothed, but small irregular teeth or shallow indentations may be present.

**ENTIRE BROAD EVERGREEN LEAVES**—up to twice as long as broad. Varying in shape from kidney-shaped, heart-shaped, rounded, oval, ovate, to elliptic; with apex acute, obtuse, or notched, and base heart-shaped, rounded, straight or wedge-shaped—but all with margins without regular teeth or indentations.

**TOOTHED BROAD EVERGREEN LEAVES**—shape varying as in previous category, but margins toothed or indented. Teeth coarse or fine, rounded, saw-toothed, or spiny; indentations to less than $\frac{1}{4}$ the distance from the edge of the blade to the mid-vein.

**SCALE-LIKE EVERGREEN LEAVES**—tiny triangular or ovate leaves, not more than 5 mm long, with a broad base closely or partly encircling the twigs so that twigs appear green and cord-like. Scale leaves often in ranks, making twigs triangular, rectangular, etc.

**ENTIRE NARROW DECIDUOUS LEAVES**—more than twice as long as wide. Ranging from very long and thin to oblong-ovate. Blade apex acute, blunt, or notched; base wedge-shaped to heart-shaped. Margins without conspicuous teeth or indentations. The distinction between this category and the next is often blurred, and leaves of both categories may occur on an individual plant or on different plants of the same species under different conditions.

**ENTIRE BROAD DECIDUOUS LEAVES**—less than twice as long as wide. Leaves ranging from ovate, elliptic, heart-shaped, rounded, to kidney-shaped all fall into this category. Margins without teeth or indentations. Blade apex and base varies as in the previous category.

**TOOTHED NARROW DECIDUOUS LEAVES**—more than twice as long as wide. Margins with coarse or fine, acute or blunt teeth, or double-toothed; or with shallow indentations to less than $\frac{1}{4}$ the distance from the edge of the blade to the mid-vein. Shape varying as in *Entire Narrow Deciduous Leaves* category.

**TOOTHED BROAD DECIDUOUS LEAVES**—less than twice as long as wide. With teeth or indentations as in the previous category; shape varying as in *Entire Broad Deciduous Leaves* category.

**PALMATELY-LOBED LEAVES**—deciduous or evergreen. Shallowly or deeply divided into 3, 4, 5, or 7 lobes, the lobes often getting progressively larger from base to apex, or the middle lobe longer and more deeply divided than the remainder. The lobes may be further toothed or cut into smaller lobes. Leaves lobed to less than $\frac{1}{4}$ of the distance to the mid-vein are not included in this category.

**PINNATELY-LOBED LEAVES**—deciduous or evergreen. Margins of leaves deeply indented (to more than $\frac{1}{4}$ of the distance to the mid-vein) with opposite pairs of rounded or pointed lobes, which themselves may be further toothed or lobed. Leaves deeply indented, almost to the mid-vein, are included in this category; but if they are cut into segments which are separated from each other where they meet the mid-vein they are *Pinnately-Compound*.

**TRIFOLIATE LEAVES**—deciduous or evergreen. With three stalked or stalkless leaflets, which may themselves be further toothed or lobed. For the identification of a leaflet see under *Pinnately-Compound*.

**PALMATELY-COMPOUND LEAVES**—deciduous or evergreen. With 5, 7, or more separate stalked or stalkless leaflets borne at the end of the leaf stalk. For the identification of a leaflet see under *Pinnately-Compound*.

**PINNATELY-COMPOUND LEAVES**—deciduous or evergreen. With pairs of leaflets arising from a central stalk or *rachis*—the continuation of the leaf stalk. Leaflets stalked or stalkless, toothed or lobed; leaves with or without a terminal leaflet. To distinguish a leaflet from a true leaf, look at the junction of the stalk with the stem or *rachis*. True leaves have a bud in this axil, sometimes very small and difficult to see, and the base of the leaf stalk may be swollen or enlarged bearing scale-like or leafy stipules; the stem bearing the leaves ends in a bud. Leaflets where they join the rachis have no buds or stipules, and the end of the rachis terminates in a leaflet, or in a sterile tip, or tendril.

**TWICE-PINNATE LEAVES**—deciduous or evergreen. With the leaflets of a pinnate leaf themselves pinnate. From the *rachis*—the continuation of the leaf stalk—arise pairs of side stalks or *pinnae,* which bear pairs of often numerous small leaflets which may be entire, toothed, or lobed.

**LEAFLESS SWITCH-LIKE OR SUCCULENT PLANTS WITH GREEN STEMS.** Switch-like plants have usually numerous slender, erect, green branches. At certain times of the year on new shoots they may have small entire or trifoliate leaves, but these may soon fall and for most of the year the twigs may be leafless. Succulent plants also may have small, often fleshy leaves which soon fall, and green, fleshy, swollen, sometimes flattened stems. In both cases the stems photosynthesize, taking over from the leaves the work of manufacturing food for the plant.

NORTH may include Great Britain as well as Scandinavia and the Low Countries.

NORTH AND CENTRAL

CENTRAL often covers the Pyrenees, Apennines, Carpathians, and Macedonian highlands, as well as the Alps and the intervening highlands and lowlands.

WEST AND SOUTH-WEST may include Britain, France and Italy as well as the Iberian peninsula.

EAST AND SOUTH-EAST may take in Italy, Austria, Hungary and Romania as well as the Balkans and the Greek islands.

SOUTH AND MEDITERRANEAN may include the southern Alps and Carpathians.

SOUTH AND CENTRAL

WIDESPREAD AND THROUGHOUT often excludes the peripheral south-west, south-east and far north.

# Glossary

**adpressed**  Pressed flat to a surface (1).

**alternate**  Leaves placed singly, at different heights on a stem (2).

**anther**  The part of the stamen containing the pollen grains (3a).

**aril**  An appendage or outer covering of a seed which may be fleshy (4a).

**awl-shaped**  Broad-based and tapering to a sharp point (5).

**axil, axillary**  The angle between the leaf and stem; hence axillary flower or bud (6a).

**berry**  A fleshy rounded fruit, usually with hard pips or seeds (7).

**bract**  A little leaf or scale-like structure from the axil of which a flower often arises (8).

**calyx, calices**  The sepals collectively; often joined together in a tube, the calyx tube (9a).

**capsule**  A dry fruit, formed of two or more fused carpels, which splits open when ripe (10, 20).

**carpel**  One of the units of the female part of the flower; they are either separate (10a) or fused together into a fruit (38).

**catkin**  A crowded spike of tiny flowers, usually hanging and tassel-like (11).

**ciliate**  Fringed with hairs along the margin (12).

**cone**  A distinct rounded or elongated structure composed of many overlapping scales (14) which bear pollen or seeds when mature (13).

**coppiced**  Periodically cut to the ground to encourage the production of new wood.

**corolla**  The petals collectively; often joined together into a tube (9b).

**deflexed**  Bent sharply downwards (15a) = reflexed.

**drupe**  A fleshy fruit with an inner hard stone enclosing the seed (16).

**entire**  Whole; without lobes or indentations (17).

**female flowers**  Flowers with a fertile ovary but without fertile stamens (18a).

**fruit**  The ripened ovary bearing the seeds; other organs may be included (20, 21, 22, 27, 46, 55).

**gall**  A growth or protuberance formed by insects, found on any part of a plant.

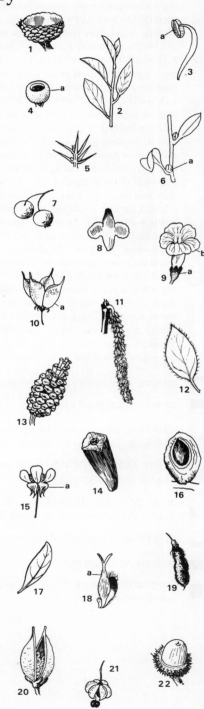

**gland, glandular**   Organs of secretion usually on the tips of the hairs; hence glandular-hairs (23).

**glaucous**   Covered or whitened with a bloom which is often waxy, thus giving the organ a bluish or greyish colour.

**inferior ovary**   Ovary situated below the petals, sepals, and stamens in the flower (24). *Half-inferior ovary* situated in a hollow, with other organs borne on the rim (25); see also *superior ovary*.

**inflorescence**   Flower branch, including the bracts, flower stalks, and flowers (26).

**involucre**   A collection of bracts, surrounding a flower, sometimes becoming woody in fruit (27a).

**lanceolate**   Lance-shaped. Narrow, pointed, broadest below the middle and regularly tapering towards the base (28).

**leaflet**   The individual part of a compound leaf which is usually leaf-like and usually possesses its own stalk (29a).

**lenticels**   Corky 'breathing pores' in bark, on twigs and some fruit.

**liana**   A woody climber usually associated with tropical forests.

**male flower**   A flower containing fertile stamens but no fertile ovary (30a).

**maquis**   A thicket of tall shrubs and scattered trees characteristically developed in a Mediterranean climate.

**needle**   A slender needle-like leaf, as found in pines (31).

**node**   A point on the stem where one or more leaves arise (32a).

**nut**   A one-seeded fruit with a hard outer covering (22, 33).

**oblanceolate, obovate**   Ob- means inverted; thus broadest part of organ nearer the apex, and not, as is usual, nearer the base (34, 35).

**opposite**   Of two organs: arising at the same level on opposite sides of the stem (36).

**ovary**   The part of the flower containing the ovules and later the seeds, usually with one or more styles and stigmas (37a, 38).

**ovate**   With an oval outline broader towards the base than the apex, and round-ended (39).

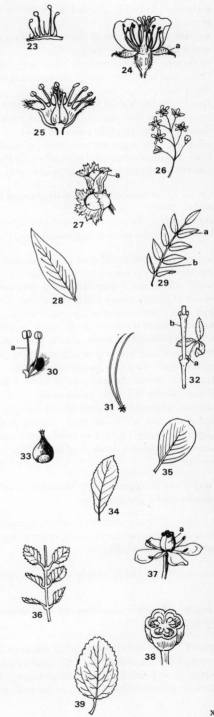

**palmate**   Lobed or divided in a palm- or hand-like manner (40).

**peltate**   A flat organ attached to its stalk on the underside not on the margin (41).

**pericarp**   Wall of the fruit, often with outer part fleshy and inner part stony, surrounding the seed or seeds (42a).

**petal**   An individual member of the inner set of sterile organs surrounding the sexual parts of the flower, usually brightly coloured (43a).

**pinnate**   The regular arrangement of leaflets in rows on either side of the stalk or *rachis* (29); thus also *twice-pinnate* (44), *pinnately-lobed* (45).

**rachis**   Continuation of leaf stalk bearing the leaflets (29b).

**receptacle**   The uppermost part of the flower stalk which bears the parts of the flower (46a).

**scale**   Any thin dry flap of tissue; usually a modified or degenerate leaf (48a); also see *cone* (47).

**seed**   Contained within the ovary, produced as a result of fertilization—consists of a coat, an embryo, and food reserves, and is capable of germination (49).

**sepal**   One of the outer set of sterile organs surrounding the sexual parts, usually green and protecting in bud, rarely coloured and petal-like (24a).

**spathulate**   Spoon or paddle-shaped (50).

**stamen**   One of the male reproductive organs of the flower, which bears the pollen (30a).

**stipule, stipulate**   A scale-like or leaf-like appendage at the base of the leaf stalk; usually paired (51a).

**superior ovary**   Ovary situated on the receptacle above the stamens, petals, and sepals (52a); see also *inferior ovary*.

**twig**   The youngest woody branches, usually of the present year's growth (32b).

**umbel**   A cluster of flowers whose spreading stalks arise from the apex of the stem, resembling the spokes of an umbrella (53).

**valve**   One of the parts into which a capsule splits (54a).

**vesicle**   A membrane, often leaf-like, encircling a fruit.

**whorl**   More than two organs of the same kind arising from the same level; thus *whorled* (5).

**wing**   A dry thin expansion of an organ (55a). Also the lateral petals of the flowers of the pea family (56a).

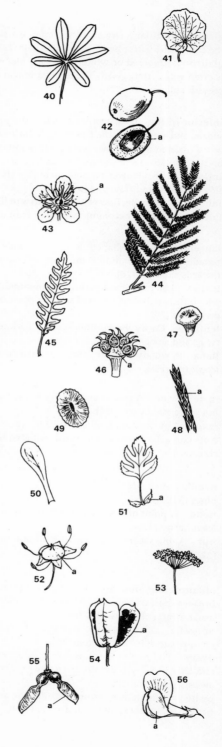

# Leaf Check List

This is not a key by elimination. Trees and bushes may occur in more than one category. Leaf sizes, shapes, etc., may overlap and occur in two or more categories.

**NARROW EVERGREEN LEAVES**—more than twice as long as wide

Firs 2; Douglas Fir 4; Hemlocks 5; Spruces 6; Cedars 10; Pines 12; Redwoods 21; Big Tree 22; Red Cedar 23; Junipers (some) 26; Yew 30; Holm Oak 52; Laurel 70; *Pittosporum* 70; Loquat 84; Cherry Laurel 98; Wattles 101; Gorse 110; Tangerine 115; Citron 115; Boxes 132; *Cistus* 144; Myrtle 147; *Eucalyptus* 148; Heathers 155; Shrubby Hare's-Ear 155; Olive 166; *Phillyrea* 167; Oleander 167; Rosemary 170; Shrubby Germander 170; Laurustinus 176; Cruel Plant 168; *Smilax* 180; Century Plant 181; *Cordyline* 181; *Dracaena* 181; *Yucca* 181; Giant Reed 182; Bamboos 182.

> **Narrow 'needle' leaves**—less than 5 mm wide
> > **Rounded, quadrangular, or triangular in section**
> > Douglas Fir; Spruces (some); Cedars; Pines; Big Tree; Red Cedar; Gorse; Heathers
> > **Flattened in section**
> > Firs; Hemlocks; Spruces (some); Redwood; Junipers (some); Yew; Rosemary
>
> **Broader leaves**—more than 5 mm wide
> > **Larger leaves**—more than 5 cm long
> > Laurel; *Pittosporum*; Loquat; Cherry Laurel; Wattles; Tangerine; Citron; *Cistus*; *Eucalyptus*; Shrubby Hare's-Ear; Olive; *Phillyrea*; Oleander; Laurustinus; *Smilax*; Century Plant; *Cordyline*; *Dracaena*; *Yucca*; Giant Reed; Bamboos
> > **Small leaves**—less than 5 cm long
> > Holm Oak; Boxes; Myrtle; Olive; *Phillyrea*; Shrubby Germander; *Smilax*
>
> **Grey-, white-, or brown-haired leaves beneath**—woolly, felty, scaly
> > Holm Oak; Loquat; *Cistus*; Olive; Rosemary; Shrubby Germander; Laurustinus
>
> **Aromatic leaves** (when crushed)
> > Firs; Douglas Fir; Spruces; Pines; Junipers; Laurel; Tangerine; Citron; *Cistus*; Myrtle; *Eucalyptus*; Rosemary

**ENTIRE BROAD EVERGREEN LEAVES**—less than twice as long as wide

Holm Oak 52; Oranges 114; Citron 115; Grapefruit 115; Cretan Maple 126; Boxes 132; Spotted Laurel 154; Ivy 154; Rhododendron 157; Greek Strawberry Tree 158; *Phillyrea* 167; Shrubby Germander 170; Laurustinus 176; Honeysuckles (some) 176; *Smilax* 180

> **Small leaves**—less than 5 cm long
> > Holm Oak; Cretan Maple; Boxes; Ivy; *Phillyrea*; Shrubby Germander; Honeysuckles

## TOOTHED BROAD EVERGREEN LEAVES

Holm Oak 52; Round-Leaved Oak 53; Cork Oak 53; Kermes Oak 54; Firethorn 86; Portugal Laurel 98; Lemon 116; Sweet Lime 116; Hollies 129; Mediterranean Buckthorn 134; Spotted Laurel 154; Strawberry Trees 158; *Phillyrea* 167

**Large leaves**—more than 5 cm long
> Portugal Laurel; Lemon; Sweet Lime; Hollies; Spotted Laurel; Strawberry Tree

## SCALE-LIKE EVERGREEN LEAVES

Cypresses 24; Lawson's Cypress 25; Western Red Cedar 26; Junipers (some) 26; Alerce 29; Tamarisks 144; German Tamarisk 146

## ENTIRE NARROW DECIDUOUS LEAVES—more than twice as long as wide

Larches 9; Swamp Cypress 22; Willows (few) 31; Pears (few) 74; Medlar 86; *Prunus webbii* 92; Brooms (some) 108; *Lygos* 109; *Coriaria* 118; Sea Buckthorn 143; Oleaster 143; Pomegranate 151; Dogwood (some) 152; *Fuchsia* 151; Azalea 157; *Diospyros* 159; Lilac 164; Privets 165; *Lycium* 171; *Cestrum* 172; Shrub Tobacco 172; Honeysuckles (some) 177; Banana 185

**Trees**—usually more than 5 m
> Larches; Swamp Cypress; Pears; Oleaster; *Diospyros*

## ENTIRE BROAD DECIDUOUS LEAVES—less than twice as long as wide

Beeches 50; Osage Orange 65; Quince 74; Pears (some) 75; Cotoneasters 85; Judas Tree 99; *Coriaria* 118; Wig Tree 119; Pistachio 121; Tatarian Maple 124; Dogwoods (some) 152; Cornelian Cherry 153; *Fuchsia* 151; *Diospyros* 159; Storax 160; Lilac 164; Silk-Vine 168; Stranglewort 169; Shrub Tobacco 172; Foxglove-Tree 173; Indian Bean-Tree 173; Honeysuckles (some) 177; Snowberry 180

**Trees**—usually more than 5 m
> Beeches; Osage Orange; Pears; Judas Tree; Tatarian Maple; *Diospyros*; Foxglove-Tree; Indian Bean-Tree

**Climbers**
> Silk-Vine; Stranglewort; Honeysuckles (some)

## TOOTHED NARROW DECIDUOUS LEAVES

Willows (many) 31; Sweet Chestnut 51; Oaks (few) 52; Almond 91; Peach 92; Cherries (some) 95; Spindles 129; *Zizyphus* 134; *Vaccinium* 158; *Buddleja* 172

**Trees**—usually more than 5 m
> White, Crack, Weeping Willows; Sweet Chestnut; Macedonian, Portuguese Oaks; Almond; Peach; Wild, Sour, Bird, Black Cherries

## TOOTHED BROAD DECIDUOUS LEAVES

Willows (some) 31; Poplars (most) 36; Birches 43; Alders 44; Hornbeams 47; Hop-Hornbeam 48; Hazels 49; Oaks (few) 52; Elms 60; *Zelkova* 63; Nettle Trees 63; Mulberries 64; Pears (some) 75; Apples 77; Whitebeams (some) 79; Snowy Mespilus 84; *Amelanchier* 85; Hawthorns (some) 87; Apricot 92; Plums 93;

Cherries (few) 95; Spindles 130; Christ's Thorn 133; Buckthorns 134; Limes 139; *Forsythia* 164; *Wigandia* 169; Wayfaring Tree 176

### Leaf-blades with heart-shaped or straight base

White, Grey, Black Poplars; Aspen; Cottonwood; Alders (few); Elms; Nettle-Trees; Mulberries; Pears (some); Apricot; Limes; *Wigandia*; Wayfaring Tree

### Leaf-blades with rounded or wedge-shaped base

Willows; Poplars (some); Birches; Alders (most); Hornbeams; Hop-Hornbeam; Hazels; Oaks; Elms; *Zelkova;* Nettle Trees; White Mulberry; Barberry; Pears (some); Apples; Whitebeams; Snowy Mespilus; *Amelanchier;* Hawthorns; Plums; Cherries; Spindles; Christ's Thorn; Buckthorns; *Forsythia*

 **PALMATELY-LOBED LEAVES**—deciduous or evergreen; 3–5–7 lobed

Poplars 37; White Mulberry 65; Paper Mulberry 65; Fig 66; *Clematis cirrhosa* 68; Tulip Tree 69; Planes 71; Nine Bark 74; *Malus trilobata* 78; *Malus florentina* 78; Wild Service Tree 80; Hawthorns (most) 87; Castor Oil 113; Maples (most) 122; Sycamore 124; Vines 137; Virginia Creeper 138; *Hibiscus* 142; Ivy 154; Guelder Rose 175

### Leaves distinctly hairy beneath

White, Grey Poplars; Paper Mulberry; Fig; Nine Bark; *Malus florentina*; Wild Service Tree; Hawthorns (some); *Acer obtusatum*; Vine; *Hibiscus*

 **PINNATELY-LOBED LEAVES**—deciduous or evergreen

Oaks (most) 52; Whitebeams (some) 79; *Solanum* 171

 **TRIFOLIATE LEAVES**—deciduous or evergreen

Bean Trefoil 106; Laburnums 106; Spiny Brooms 107; Brooms 108; *Petteria* 110; Gorse 110; *Adenocarpus* 111; Tree Medick 113; Hop Tree 116; Pistachio 121; Jasmine (some) 164

 **PALMATELY-COMPOUND LEAVES**—deciduous or evergreen

Tree Lupin 111; Horse-Chestnut 128; *Parthenocissus* (some) 138; Chaste Tree 169; Fan-Palms 184

 **PINNATELY-COMPOUND LEAVES**—deciduous or evergreen

Walnuts 41; Bitternut 42; Hickories 42; Wing-Nut 43; Clematis 67; Service Tree 79; Rowan 80; Carob 100; Honey-Locust 101; Pagoda Tree 105; False Acacia 111; Wisteria 112; Bladder Sennas 112; False Indigo 113; Tree of Heaven 117; Sumach 119; Terebinth 120; Mastic Tree 120; Pepper Tree 121; Box-Elder 127; Bladdernut 131; Ashes 161; Jasmines (some) 164; Elders 174; Palms (some) 183

### Leaflets many—10 or more

Black Walnut; Wing-Nut; Service Tree; Rowan; Honey-Locust; False Acacia; Wisteria (some); Bladder Sennas (some); False Indigo; Tree of Heaven; Sumach; Mastic Tree (some); Pepper Tree; Ashes; Palms (some)

**TWICE-PINNATE LEAVES**—deciduous or evergreen

Fragrant Clematis 67; Honey-Locust 101; Wattles, Mimosa (some), 101; Persian Acacia 105; Persian Lilac 117

○ **LEAFLESS SWITCH-PLANTS or SUCCULENTS with GREEN STEMS**

Spiny Brooms 107; Brooms 108; *Lygos* 109; Gorse 110; *Opuntia* 146

# Acknowledgements

A volume of this nature could not be undertaken without the help and collaboration of a considerable number of people or without the facilities available in our great national collections, surely unrivalled in the world. We would like to thank the Director of the Royal Botanic Gardens, Kew, the Keeper of the Herbarium and his staff for their unfailing kindness and help.

For their assistance in many ways we are also indebted to the following: to Miss P. Halliday, Anthony Everard and Mrs Bateman for collecting specimens to be painted; to Mrs S. Bosence, Mrs M. Briggs, Miss D. S. F. Williams, and R. A. Mackilligin for information provided towards the appendix 'Uses to Man'; to Mrs K. Cooke for most painstaking typing and for compiling the index; and to C. R. Lancaster, Curator of the Hillier Garden and Arboretum, for his continuing co-operation and advice throughout the preparation of this book.

The photographs are largely our own, taken in the field or in cultivation, and we should like to record our gratitude for the opportunities provided by such great collections of living plants available to the public at Kew, Wakehurst, Bedgebury National Pinetum, Alice Holt Forest Research Station, the Royal Horticultural Society Gardens at Wisley, and the Hillier Garden and Arboretum. We would also like to thank the following friends most warmly for the loan of transparencies of species that we have had difficulty in photographing ourselves: B. C. Fleming-Williams 29d, 66d, 66e, 113e, 115b, 115e, 116c, 116d, 121a, 146b, 181c, 181e; C. R. Lancaster 3a, 4a, 6d, 37a, 114b, 118a, 125c, 126c; Č. Šilić 33b, 83a, 83b, 95e, 130d, 131b, 134d, 153d; Dr M. Fischer 19b, 131a, 165a; Sir C. Barclay 126e, 169d, 183e, 184a; Prof. A. Baytop 159b; Mrs J. I. Byatt 89a; R. C. Crow 109b; W. R. Sykes 104c; Mrs A. Woodbridge 142c.

# PINE FAMILY                    Pinaceae

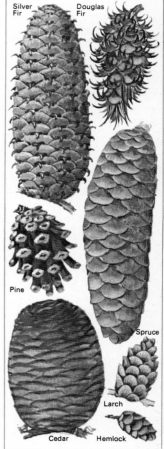

An ancient and very important family of trees which form dominant forests clothing large tracts of the cooler parts of the northern hemisphere, and mountains further south. Distinguished by its needle-like leaves, and two kinds of cones formed of spirally arranged scales (2), (8). Female cones (4) woody; seeds (7) borne on the upper sides of scales (8). Male cones (1) short-lived, with pollen sacs borne on the underside of scales (2). Seeds and pollen are usually winged. Leaves single (3) or clustered (5), (6). There are about 210 world species; 18 are native to Europe, many more have been introduced for timber and ornament.

| Key to PINE Family | PINACEAE |
|---|---|
| 1 Leaves all single (3). | |
|   2 Leaves borne on peg-like projections. | |
|     3 Leaves shortly stalked (3); cones small, pendulous, to 2.5 cm. | **Hemlocks** (p5) |
|     3 Leaves stalkless; cones medium to large, pendulous, 3 cm or more. | **Spruces** (p6–9) |
|   2 Leaves not borne on peg-like projections. | |
|     4 Leaf-scar circular, flat; cones erect, breaking up when ripe leaving the central axis. | **Silver Firs** (p2–4) |
|     4 Leaf-scar elliptic, slightly raised; cones pendulous, falling intact. | **Douglas Fir** (p4) |
| 1 Leaves in clusters, at least on older shoots (5), (6). | |
|   5 Leaves in clusters of 2, 3, or 5 (5); cones not breaking up when ripe. | **Pines** (p12–20) |
|   5 Leaves many in each cluster (6). | |
|     6 Leaves deciduous; cones small, not breaking up when ripe. | **Larches** (p9–10) |
|     6 Leaves evergreen; cones large, breaking up when ripe leaving the central axis. | **Cedars** (p10–11) |

Note: leaves = needles.

## Silver Fir
*Abies alba*

  † *

A slender conical tree to 50 m, forming dominant forests, from 800–1900 m, in the mountains of central Europe extending from the Pyrenees to Bulgaria. It has a smooth grey, blistered trunk when young, and spreading whorled branches. Needles thick, flexible, notched at apex (3), arranged in two ranks. Twigs characteristically covered with pale brown hairs; buds not resinous. Cones erect, green then orange-brown, 10–20 cm: when ripe disintegrating into fan-shaped scales (1) and longer toothed bracts with recurved tips (2). The central axis (4) remains on the tree. An important timber tree, no longer planted in Britain because of greenfly attack and damage from late frosts.

King Boris's Fir, *A. borisii-regis*, probably a hybrid, is found in the mountains of the Balkans. It has acute needles, densely hairy twigs, and resinous buds.

## Greek Fir
*Abies cephalonica*

Replaces the Silver Fir in the higher mountains of Greece from 750–1700 m, where it forms forests. Conical tree very like the former, but distinguished by its rigid prickly-pointed needles which radiate from all round the hairless twigs, without a parting above. This, and the Spanish Fir are the only two species which have needles radiating all round the stem, the others have a parting. The erect

a

b

c

d

e

fruiting cones are golden-brown, 12–16 cm, with protruding, reflexed, triangular bracts. Its timber is similar to that of the Silver Fir, though it is used only locally. It is sometimes grown for ornament.

a

## Caucasian Fir
*Abies nordmanniana*

 ‡

A native tree of Turkey eastwards, planted for timber in several countries of C. Europe. Needles firm and leathery, 1.5–3.5 cm, densely arranged, forward-directed and notched at tip and grooved above. Buds (1) not resinous; twigs brown. Cones dark brown, resin covered, 12–18 cm; scales projecting and with a down-curved tip.

## Spanish or Hedgehog Fir
*Abies pinsapo*

A rare tree of limestone mountains near Ronda in S. Spain, still existing in 3 forest areas. Like the Greek Fir with rigid needles arranged all round stem, but needles short, 1–1.5 cm, blunt or acute, not prickly-tipped. Cones cylindrical, tapering above, bracts not exposed between scales. Sometimes planted for timber in central Europe.

b

c

d

×⅘ Caucasian Fir

buds

×1½

×1

Spanish Fir

×2

3

# PINE FAMILY

## Noble Fir
*Abies procera (nobilis)*

A conical, very handsome tree distinguished by its silvery-grey 'elephant-hide' trunk, and its bluish-grey foliage. Needles leathery, blunt, 1–3.5 cm, densely crowded. Cones very large, up to 20 cm long. Native of N. America; planted for timber in N. and W. Europe.

## Giant Fir
*Abies grandis*

Probably the fastest growing conifer introduced to Europe, increasing as much as 1.5 m each year. A N. American tree; planted for timber in N. and C. Europe. Distinguished by its shining, soft, two-ranked, comb-like needles which have an orange-like aroma when crushed, borne on olive-green, downy twigs. Cones small, 5–10 cm; bracts not showing.

## Douglas Fir
*Pseudotsuga menziesii*

Distinguished from all other conifers by the drooping oval-cylindrical cones (3) which have conspicuous, narrow, three-pointed bracts (2), much longer than the broad scales (1). One of the tallest trees recorded in Europe (in Britain to 55 m) despite its relatively late introduction in 1827. In the Rocky Mountains it grows to 100 m. Probably the most extensively planted conifer in Europe. The

needles are solitary, flexible, 2–
3.5 cm, and leave an elliptical
scar (4). Twigs finely hairy and
buds (5) spindle-shaped, recalling those of beech; the foliage is
sweetly aromatic when crushed.
Young cones (a) reddish-brown.
The bark is characteristically
purplish-brown, with wide,
deep, corky fissures on old
trees. Its timber, known as
Oregon or Columbian Pine, is
light, strong, and durable.

## Western Hemlock
*Tsuga heterophylla*

Hemlocks are distinguished by
their flattened, short-stalked
needles which are variable in
length, and by their small,
smooth, pendulous, ovoid cones.
Western Hemlock is a tall, graceful conical tree to 48 m, with
lustrous aromatic foliage, and
drooping leading shoots. It is
native of western N. America;
often planted for timber in
N.–W. Europe.

## Eastern Hemlock
*Tsuga canadensis*

A N. American tree like the preceding but with several trunks
branching from the base and a
broad conical crown. Buds
ovoid (2), not globular (1), and
needles somewhat tapered (2),
and with 2 narrower white
bands beneath, not parallel-
sided (1). Cones terminal, 1.5–2
cm. Occasionally planted for
timber, giving a high yield of
inferior quality.

# PINE FAMILY

## Norway Spruce
*Picea abies*

An important forest-forming tree of the mountains of Europe, from Lapland to the Balkans; this is the familiar Christmas tree. Like all spruces, it is distinguished by the peg-like projections (1), (2) from which the needles arise, and which remain after the needles fall, resulting in twigs which are very rough to the touch. Needles dark green, four-sided (3), sharp-pointed, 1–2.5 cm; twigs reddish-brown. Male cones terminal. Female cones (4) pendulous, 10–18 cm long, falling intact. The rusty brown, smooth bark is characteristic; on older trees it is dark purplish and cracked into small rounded plates. A most important timber tree, extensively planted in Europe. The timber is known as white deal or white wood.

a

b

bud

1
×1½

2
×1½

3
×10

4

c

## Serbian Spruce
*Picea omorika*

A very slender, spire-like tree of mountains of the Drina River region, Yugoslavia. Needles flattened, with 2 white bands beneath, and a broad blunt tip (see p. 8). Cones small, 3–6 cm. Bark orange-brown, flaking. Sometimes grown for timber in N. Europe; an ornamental tree which grows well in Britain.

d

e

## Sitka Spruce
*Picea sitchensis*

 ‡

A tall, graceful, conical tree, growing to 50 m or more, with arching branches. Distinguished by its flattened needles, similar to Serbian Spruce, but stiff and prickly-pointed (see p. 8). Cones 6–10 cm, very distinctive with crinkled margins to the scales. The bark of young trees is greyish but soon becomes purplish, and flakes into small plates. A native of N. America, now widely planted in N., W., and C. Europe as an important timber tree and one of the fastest growing in W. Europe, increasing 1–1.5 m each year. The wood is light, fine-grained, and strong.

## Oriental Spruce
*Picea orientalis*

 ‡

A forest tree of Turkey and the Caucasus, large, conical, densely branched, growing to 40 m. It has the shortest needles (see p. 8) of any spruce, only 6–10 mm long, four-sided, blunt, shining dark green and close-pressed to the hairy, pale brown twigs beneath. The young male cones (d) are at first red and turn yellow when ripe. Female cones (e) 6–9 cm, narrow tapering, with rounded scales, at first purple

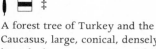

# PINE FAMILY

then brown. Occasionally planted for timber on a small scale in Belgium, Austria, and Italy, and frequently planted for ornament in Great Britain.

## Engelmann Spruce
*Picea engelmannii*

A mountain forest tree of N. America with unpleasant-smelling foliage when bruised, like White Spruce (below). Differing in its minutely hairy, greyish-yellow young twigs and its more rigid needles 1.5–2.5 cm, either green or glaucous. Planted for timber in N. Europe, and slope-conservation in the Alps.

## White Spruce
*Picea glauca*

A native tree of N. America best recognized by its slender, stiff, grey or pale bluish-green needles, and its mousy smelling foliage when crushed. Needles 8–18 mm, four-sided; twigs shiny, hairless, whitish or pinkish. Cones 3.5–5 cm, scales few, loosely overlapping. Sometimes planted for timber mainly in N. Europe.

a

b

c

d

×2
×4
×1½
Serbian Spruce

×1
Sitka Spruce
×1½

×1½
Oriental Spruce
×1

×2
White Spruce
×1½

×2
×1½
Blue Spruce

**Blue or Colorado Spruce**
*Picea pungens*

A handsome decorative tree,
particularly the various glaucous forms. Distinguished by its
stout, four-sided, prickly-pointed needles, its hairless yellow-
brown twigs (see p. 8), and the
reflexed tips of the bud scales.
Male cones (a) red. A native of
southern N. America; sometimes planted for timber in N.
and C. Europe.

**European Larch**
*Larix decidua*

The only native European conifer which sheds its leaves annually. A beautiful conical tree
to 35 m with down-sweeping
branches, long pendulous twigs,
breaking into bright clear green
in spring and turning golden-
yellow in autumn. Twigs (2)
straw-coloured and hairless.
Needles on young twigs single,
but older twigs have bosses of
30–40 needles (3). Male cones
(1) globular, 0.5–1 cm; young female cones (4) reddish, attractive
and flower-like. Mature cones
(5) 2–3.5 cm, with broad rounded cone scales which are straight
or incurved. A native of the
mountains of C. Europe from the
Alps to the W. Carpathians.
Also planted further west and
north for its valuable timber
which is stronger than that of
most conifers.

# PINE FAMILY

## Japanese Larch
*Larix kaempferi (leptolepis)*

Distinguished by its reddish-violet or orange-red often bloomed twigs; its wider grey-green needles, and its rosette-like cones (1) with scales which curve outwards. A native of Japan; commonly planted as a tougher, faster-growing tree than the European Larch.
The hybrid Dunkeld Larch (3) grows even faster and is often now planted instead.

## Dahurian Larch
*Larix gmelinii*

A Siberian tree which is planted for timber in N. Europe. Distinguished by its bright grass-green needles which appear very early in the year; its small cones (2) 2–2.5 cm which are hairless outside.
Also planted in the north is the Siberian Larch, *L. russica*, which has cones about 3.5 cm and finely hairy cone scales (4) and twigs.

## Atlas Cedar
*Cedrus atlantica*

The true cedars are unique in having evergreen needles in clusters on side shoots, as well as barrel-shaped cones which shatter when ripe. There are four species spreading from the Mediterranean to the Himalaya. The Atlas Cedar grows in the mountains of N. Africa where its durable aromatic timber is much prized. Sometimes planted for timber in S. Europe, also for ornament elsewhere, particular-

Japanese Larch
1 ×1½ ×1½ 2
Dahurian Larch
3 Hybrid Dunkeld Larch ×1½ ×1½ 4 Siberian Larch ×1½

ly the glaucous varieties. The tree has characteristically a broad conical form with widely spaced, ascending branches which bear level 'plates' of foliage. Needles 1–3 cm, green or glaucous. Male cones (p. 10d) 3–5 cm, conical, Female cones (p. 10e) 3–8 cm, flat or sunken at apex, disintegrating into fan-shaped scales, winged seeds and leaving a central axis.

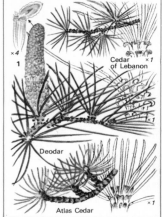

a

### Cedar of Lebanon
*Cedrus libani*

Closely related to Atlas Cedar but native of the E. Mediterranean in Turkey and the Lebanon. Distinguished by its hairless young twigs, its dark green needles, and its larger female cones 7–12 cm long. Very massive, often flat-topped trees with level upper branches. Frequently planted as an ornamental tree.

b

c

### Deodar
*Cedrus deodara*

Distinguished by its pendulous leading shoots; longer needles 2–5 cm, and its large female cones 8–12 cm with rounded apices. Male cones (1) 5–12 cm, cylindrical. Twigs densely hairy and needles usually green, sometimes glaucous. Native of W. Himalaya forming forests between 2,000–3,000 m. Sometimes planted for timber in S. Europe.

d

e

11

# PINE FAMILY

## Key to PINES (*Pinus*)

1 Leaves in clusters of 2 (10).
  2 Seeds wingless or wings less       Stone (p14)
    than 1 mm (5).
  2 Seeds with well-developed
    wings (6).
    3 Twigs grey in first year.
      4 Leaves less than 1 mm wide;    Aleppo (p12)
        coasts and dry hills.
      4 Leaves more than 1 mm      **Bosnian** (p13), **Balkan**
        wide; mountains.             (p14)
    3 Twigs not grey in first year.
      5 Buds not resinous; bud       **Calabrian** (p13),
        scales with recurved apexes (9).   **Maritime** (p15)
      5 Bud scales resinous; bud
        scales not recurved at apex (8).
        6 Cones asymmetrical or     **Lodgepole** (p17), **Jack**
          strongly curved (3).       (p18)
        6 Cones more or less sym-
          metrical (2).
          7 Leaves bluish-green.     Scots (p15)
          7 Leaves bright green, or   **Mountain, Dwarf Moun-**
            light, or dark green.    **tain** (p17), **Black** (p16)
1 Leaves not in clusters of 2.
  8 Leaves mostly in clusters of 3 (11).
    9 Leaves stout, rigid; cone     **Western Yellow** (p19)
      scales with a point (7).
    9 Leaves slender, flexible; cone   **Monterey** (p18), **Canary**
      scales without a point (13).    **Island** (p18)
  8 Leaves mostly in clusters of 5 (12).
    10 Cones egg-shaped, 5–8 cm,   **Arolla** (p19)
       erect (4).
    10 Cones cylindrical, 8–20 cm,   **Macedonian, Weymouth,**
       mostly pendulous (1).     **Himalayan Blue** (p20)

## Aleppo Pine
*Pinus halepensis*

▮ ▢ *

A familiar and widespread tree
of the hotter and drier soils of
the Mediterranean coast and
hills inland. A small, often
gnarled and twisted tree to 20 m
with reddish-brown, deeply fissured bark in older specimens.
Easily distinguished by its pale
grey, almost white twigs and
branches, its long very slender
needles, and its shining reddish
cones. Needles clear green, flex-

a

b

12

ible, curved, 6–15 cm. Buds not resinous. Cones 5–12 cm, borne on short down-curved stalks, and remaining on tree for several years. One of the most resistant of trees, able to survive hot rainless summer months in an otherwise treeless landscape. It is an important soil conserver; it is tapped for resin (a) and has many uses.

## Calabrian Pine
*Pinus brutia*

Closely related to the Aleppo Pine, replacing it in the Mediterranean region from Calabria and Crete eastwards to Asia Minor where it forms open forests on coastal hills. Distinguished by its reddish-yellow or greenish first year twigs, and rigid dark green needles. Cones with short, straight (not recurved) stalks (c).

## Bosnian Pine
*Pinus leucodermis*

Two closely related pines with silvery-grey bark, grey young twigs, and large relatively broad, stiff needles, are found in the limestone mountains of the Balkan peninsula. They have medium-sized, slightly shining cones 7–8 cm, with rigid narrow points to the cone scales, dark bluish-purple when young. The Bosnian Pine is more widespread, occurring from Italy to Bulgaria. It has pale, almost

whitish twigs and stems, which remain so for several years. Needles dark green, spiny-pointed, in dense tufts at the ends of the branches. Cone scales with a recurved spiny tip. The Balkan Pine, *P. heldreichii*, has twigs which turn brown in the second year, and cone scales with a short, straight spiny tip. A small tree to 20 m with a rounded pyramidal crown, restricted to Yugoslavia, Albania, and Greece. Often not recognized as a distinct species from the Bosnian Pine.

## Stone or Umbrella Pine
*Pinus pinea*

A picturesque tree, so conspicuous during the hot dry Mediterranean summer, when its very dense umbrella-like crown gives welcome shade to man and beast alike. Though native of the western Mediterranean, it is often planted along the coast further east. Its crop of rich, oily, edible seeds (2), known as pine kernels (*pignons, piñones*, or *pinocchi*, depending on the country) are much sought after. Needles dark green, 10–20 cm, sharp-pointed. Twigs at first greyish-green; buds (3) with reflexed, white-fringed scales. Cones large, 8–14 cm by 10 cm, ovoid and symmetrical, shining brown, with domed bosses to the scales (1); seeds large, with a hard husk. The tree is very resistant to sea winds.

14

## Maritime Pine
*Pinus pinaster (maritima)*

  † *

An important native tree of the
W. Mediterranean and S. Atlantic coasts of Europe. It is also
extensively planted on poor acid
soils and sand-dunes in the S.W.
and elsewhere for shelter, soil-
conservation, and timber. A
handsome, sombre tree with
dark green leathery, rigid,
spiny-pointed needles, 10–25
cm (the longest and stoutest of
the Old World pines). Twigs
pale brown, hairless, becoming
reddish-brown. Buds (1) not
resinous. Male cones (c) numerous, clustered, short-lived. The
female cones are the longest of
all European species, up to 22
cm long, clustered and remaining on the tree several years
before opening. Resin, a most
important product, is obtained
by cutting shallow diagonal
grooves into the trunk, from
which it oozes (see p. 13a).
Periodically new cuts are made.
After 4–5 years follows a period
of rest.

## Scots Pine
*Pinus sylvestris*

  † *

This beautiful and familiar tree
is distinguished from all other
European pines by the rusty-
red, scaly branches and upper
trunk. Its blue-green foliage is
distinctive, amongst other pines.
Male cones (5) short-lived,
clustered on new shoots in early
summer. Female cones pink at
pollination, green in second
year (3), and brown in third
year (2). Seeds winged (4).
Needles flexible, twisted, 3–7 cm

long; twigs hairless, at first
greenish-yellow but becoming
greyish-brown. The Scots Pine
has the widest distribution of
any European pine but becomes
restricted to mountains in the
south. There are many different
geographical forms varying in
shape of crown, trunk, and
bark. A valuable timber
producing tree.

## Black Pines
*Pinus nigra*

  † *

A widely distributed mountain
tree of C. and S. Europe. Recognized in general by its dark,
blackish-brown, upper branches, yellowish-tawny twigs, stout
needles, and ovoid, abruptly
pointed buds. Cones tawny,
shining, 3–8 cm. There are many
geographical races, distinctive
in their own regions, but not
easily identified elsewhere.
The Austrian Pine (d), ssp. *nigra*,
is a tall, heavily branched,
gaunt, conical tree. Needles
rigid, curved, prickly-pointed.
Native from Austria to Greece.
The Pyrenean Pine (p. 17b),
ssp. *salzmannii*, is a narrow
conical tree of Spain and S.–W.
France. Needles flexible, soft-
pointed; cone small, 4–6 cm.
Corsican Pine, ssp. *laricio*, has
flexible, twisted, sage-green,
somewhat prickly-pointed
needles; cones 6–8 cm; crown
narrow-ovoid. Native of Corsica,
Sardinia, and Calabria. Dalmatian
Pine, ssp. *dalmatica*, native of
coastal Yugoslavia, has a broad
pyramidal crown, short,

a

b

Crimean Pine

Corsican Pine

Austrian Pine    Pyrenean Pine

c

d

e

rigid needles, 4–7 cm, and small cones, 3.5–4.5 cm. The Crimean Pine, ssp. *pallasiana* (a and p. 16e), has a broad crown, long, twisted, irregularly curved needles 12–18 cm, a large cone 5–12 cm. Native of the Balkans and Carpathians. Black Pines are important timber yielding trees. They are widely planted as a wind break in exposed places.

### Dwarf Mountain Pine
*Pinus mugo*

A shrubby dwarf pine with ascending branches to 3.5 m, forming thickets above the timber line in the mountains of C. Europe. Needles (2) stiff, 3–8 cm; cones (4) small, 2–5 cm; scale-tips flattish (3).
Mountain Pine, *P. uncinata*, is an erect tree to 25 m, with larger cones 5–7 cm, and scales with hooked or hooded tips (1). Spain to Alps.

### Lodgepole or Beach Pine
*Pinus contorta*

A N. American tree, sometimes planted for timber in C. and N. Europe, particularly in exposed places and in shallow soils. A small but very variable tree with dark brown bark, and twisted stunted branches. Needles twisted; buds long-conical, often twisted, resin-encrusted. Cones small 2–6 cm; scales (5) with brittle spiny tips.

a

b

c

Mountain Pine

1

×1

2

×1

3

×1

Dwarf Mountain Pine

4

bud

×1  5

young male cones

young female cones

d

17

# PINE FAMILY

## Jack Pine
*Pinus banksiana*

A very hardy, irregularly branched tree with short, broad, twisted needles. Cones borne in whorls along branches, facing forwards, small, twisted, and distorted. Cones opened by forest fires and consequently it is the first tree to recolonize burnt areas in N. America. Occasionally planted in C. Europe for timber.

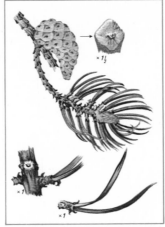

a

## Monterey Pine
*Pinus radiata*

A remarkably wind resistant tree with grass-green foliage forming a large, irregular, dense, round topped crown. Native of the Monterey Peninsula, California; often planted in W. Europe as a shelter tree by the sea. Needles in clusters of 3, soft, slender, 10–15 cm. Bark dark brown, deeply fissured. Cones large, 7–14 by 5–8 cm, often clustered, very asymmetrical, remaining on branches.

b

seed

male cones

$\times \frac{4}{5}$ cone scale

## Canary Island Pine
*Pinus canariensis*

A native of the Canary Islands; sometimes planted for timber in the Mediterranean region. A three-needled pine, identified by its very long slender needles 20–30 cm, yellow twigs, and white-fringed bud scales. Cones very large 10–20 cm, solitary or clustered. The timber is of high quality and very durable.

c

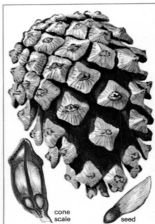

cone scale

seed

## Western Yellow Pine
### *Pinus ponderosa*

  ‡

A tall, narrow, spire-like, three-needled pine to 40 m, of N. America. Occasionally planted for timber in C. Europe. Needles 10–25 cm, stiff, curved, in tufts at the ends of stout twigs, and very aromatic. Bark with irregular 'jig-saw' scales. Cones bristly, 8–15 cm, solitary or clustered.

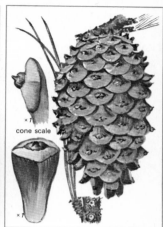

cone scale

×1

×1

a

## Arolla Pine
### *Pinus cembra*

 *

A native of the higher mountains of C. Europe found growing to nearly 3,000 m—the limit of tree growth. It is a broad, dense, conical tree, to 25 m, with stout spreading branches; bark smooth, greenish-grey, with resin blisters, later becoming rugged and scaly. Distinguished by its 5-clustered needles, contrastingly dark green outside and grey-green on the inner side, densely packed, and arising in tufts on the twigs. Twigs covered with dense orange-brown down (3). Female cones (2) at first green with a violet tinge, then purplish-brown. Scales not separating; the cone falls as a whole and the seeds are released by rotting. Seeds (1) are large and edible, with a tough outer shell. Sometimes planted for timber in Scandinavia.

b

c

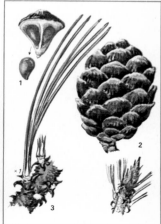

1

2

×1

3

# PINE FAMILY

**Macedonian Pine**
*Pinus peuce*

**Himalayan Blue Pine** (c)
*Pinus wallichiana*

The former is a tall, stately, narrow pyramidal tree to 30 m of the mountains of S. Yugoslavia, Albania and W. Bulgaria. A five-needled pine, it is distinguished from all other European pines by its long cylindrical cones. Needles dark blue-green, slender but rigid, densely crowded and forward-pointing. Young twigs smooth, hairless, soon shining green. Cones solitary or clustered, 8–15 cm, usually pendulous, very resinous, becoming dark reddish-brown. Bark grey or brown, remaining smooth for a long time, then shallowly fissured.

The closely related Himalayan Blue Pine or Bhutan Pine, differs in having flexible pendulous needles and straight, not curved, cones 15–25 cm. A native of the Himalaya which is occasionally planted for timber.

**Weymouth Pine**
*Pinus strobus*

Known as White Pine in its native N. America, where it forms extensive forests; planted for timber particularly in C. Europe. Like the previous five-needled pines, having long pendulous cones, but distinguished by its horizontal masses of bluish-green foliage, and young twigs with fine reddish-brown hairs (1).

a

b

c

$\times \frac{2}{3}$

$\times 1$

seed

$\times 1$

cone
scale $\times 1$

$\times 1$

1

$\times 1$

d

# SWAMP CYPRESS FAMILY

## Taxodiaceae

This family may be said to be an assemblage of 'living-fossil trees', all that remains of widely dispersed, ancient types of woody plants known otherwise only as fossils. It consists of 10 distinct genera and 16 living species, of which the Dawn Redwood *Metasequoia* was discovered as recently as 1941 in W. China. Botanically the family is distinguished by its woody female cones, in which the scales are formed by the fusion of both bract and cone scale and appear double; they bear 2–9 seeds each. Male cones, small, of spiral scales each with 2–8 pollen sacs. Trees one-sexed. Leaves spirally arranged, awl-like, or flattened, evergreen or deciduous.

Californian Redwood

Swamp Cypress

Big Tree

Japanese Cedar

## Californian Redwood

*Sequoia sempervirens*

  ‡

Considered to be the tallest tree in the world, recorded to a height of 112 m in the forests of the fog-belt of the Pacific coast of America. It may live for 1,000 years or more, and it can regenerate from suckers—an unusual feature. A straight tree with a narrow columnar crown and long spreading or drooping branches. Bark very distinctive, thick, spongy, 'punchable'; trunk buttressed at the base. Leaves flattened, yew-like, in two ranks (3) on lateral twigs, awl-shaped and incurved on main shoots. Male cones (1) terminal. Young female cones (4) with bristly-tipped scales; mature cones (2) woody; seeds winged, 3–5 on each scale. An important timber tree in America. Occasionally planted for timber in Europe.

a

b

c

male

×6

×3

1

2

×2/8

×4

3

4

×2

female

×4

# SWAMP CYPRESS FAMILY

## Big Tree, Wellingtonia
### *Sequoiadendron giganteum*

 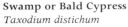 ‡

Probably the largest but not the tallest tree in the world, capable of living for 3,000 years and weighing 1,500 tons. The famous big tree forests were discovered as late as 1841 in the mountains of California. Introduced to Europe in 1853, trees of over 50 m with a girth of nearly 7 m have already been recorded in Britain. A majestic tree with a symmetrical conical form, dark green foliage, down-sweeping branches, and massive rufous trunk. Recognized by its awl-shaped, triangular-sectioned needles (2) which are arranged all round and cover the twigs. Male cones (1) clustered. Female cones (3) borne at the ends of the branches, ovoid, with 15–20 scales. The timber of American trees is very durable, but European grown timber is too soft. Often planted for ornament, and occasionally for timber in C. Europe.

## Swamp or Bald Cypress
### *Taxodium distichum*

A graceful conical tree, with light feathery foliage, native of the Mississippi region of America, which thrives by water in Europe. A unique conifer in having domed breathing roots known as 'cypress-knees' which rise above water-level and enable the tree to survive in waterlogged places. Unusual in being deciduous, and in autumn shedding whole side shoots with leaves attached (6) leaving bare twigs (7). Needles flat, two-ranked on side shoots, which are likewise two-ranked. Male cones (5) in long, often pendulous cluster. Female cones (4) (often on different trees), solitary, 1.5–3 cm; scales bearing 2 three-sided seeds. Bark reddish-brown, fibrous, and peeling in strips. Sometimes planted for timber in alluvial soils in S. Europe.

a             b

### Japanese Red Cedar
*Cryptomeria japonica*

Distinguished by its spreading, awl-shaped needles, arranged all round the twigs, and by its cones. Cone scales 20–30, each with 4–6 straight or curved spiny tips. A narrow conical tree to 37 m with a rounded apex and reddish-brown bark flaking into long fibres. Native of Japan; sometimes grown in Europe for ornament and occasionally for timber.

c

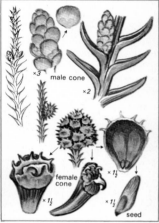

×3   male cone   ×2

female cone

×1½   ×1½   ×1½

seed

## CYPRESS FAMILY      Cupressaceae

Botanically distinguished by its cones, with scales arranged in opposite pairs at right angles to each other. Leaves of two kinds: 'juvenile leaves', needle-shaped, spreading outwards, arranged spirally which are often replaced in older plants by scale-like leaves which are closely pressed to the twig, and arranged in ranks. In consequence, twigs of some cypresses and junipers are almost indistinguishable from each other. The unique cones of junipers are berry-like, somewhat fleshy, with scales fused together, and contain several seeds. The remaining genera have small woody cones. There are about 130 species in the world — one cypress and 8 junipers are native in Europe.

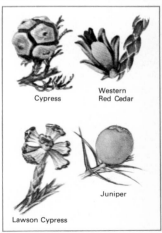

Cypress

Western Red Cedar

Lawson Cypress

Juniper

## CYPRESS FAMILY

### Italian or Funeral Cypress
*Cupressus sempervirens*

  *

A native tree of Greece and
Crete, but commonly planted for
ornament in the Mediterranean
region. Its dark slim columnar
form is often the only vertical
feature in an otherwise horizontal landscape of flat-roofed
houses and far-off sea. Slender
closely-branched forms (b) are
more commonly cultivated; but
forms with wide-spreading
crowns typical of wild plants
are also grown (c). Cypresses can
be distinguished by their globular female cones (1), with flat-
topped pentagonal scales. Male
cones (2) tiny, terminal. Leaves
(3) scale-like, only 1 mm long,
pressed flat and completely
covering the twigs, those on
leading shoots longer. Cypress
forests still exist in the mountains of Crete. Its timber is
durable, strong and fragrant,
and was much in demand in
antiquity.

### Monterey Cypress
*Cupressus macrocarpa*

  ‡

Very like Italian Cypress but
foliage bright green, lemon-
scented when crushed. Scale-
leaves longer, 1–2 mm, and ripe
cones brown not greyish (p.25).
A quick growing, salt-resistant
tree, often planted by the sea in
S. and W. Europe for shelter,
and sometimes for timber.
Native of California.

## Mexican Cypress
*Cupressus lusitanica*

A Mexican tree sometimes grown for timber and ornament in S. Europe. Distinguished by its sharp pointed scale-leaves free from the twigs at their tips. Young cones glaucous, shining brown at maturity, and scales with prominent points. A tree with drooping branches and twigs, becoming flat-topped with age.

## Lawson Cypress
*Chamaecyparis lawsoniana*

The 'false' cypresses are difficult to distinguish from the true cypresses but false cypress twigs are in flattened horizontal sprays, and their cones are rarely more than 1 cm in diameter and ripen in one year. Lawson Cypress is a massive tree to 38 m, often forked, with a graceful conical outline, and feathery tufts of bright green or greyish foliage which smell of parsley when crushed. Scale-leaves (3) triangular, arranged in 4 ranks, those of the lateral ranks larger. Twigs regularly branched in flattened, fern-like sprays. Male cones (1) terminal; female cones (2) about 8 mm when ripe (4). Seeds (5) broadly winged. There are many cultivated varieties, with golden or blue-green foliage, and erect, slender, or bushy forms which can easily be propagated by cuttings. A valuable native N. American timber tree; widely planted in Europe for timber, shelter, and ornament.

a

b

c

d

# CYPRESS FAMILY

## Western Red Cedar
*Thuja plicata*

  ‡

A dense, narrow, spire-like tree to 41 m, with fern-like foliage with a strong, fruity, resinous smell when crushed. Cones (1) distinctive, with 5–6 pairs of thin, overlapping, spreading scales. Scale-leaves (2) white-marked below, in four ranks. An important native N. American timber tree; planted for timber and shelter in Europe, and sometimes naturalized.

a

## Key to JUNIPERS (*Juniperus*)

1 Leaves all needle-like; cones axillary.
  2 Leaves with 2 pale bands above. **Prickly** (p27), **Syrian** (p27)
  2 Leaves with 1 pale band above. **Common** (p26)
1 Leaves mostly scale-like; cones terminal.
  3 Scale-leaves with narrow papery border; ripe cones reddish. **Phoenician** (p28)
  3 Scale-leaves without border; cones purple or blackish.
    4 Ripe cones 7–12 mm. **Spanish** (p28) **Stinking** (p28), **Grecian** (p29)
    4 Ripe cones 4–6 mm. **Savin** (p28), **Pencil Cedar** (p29)

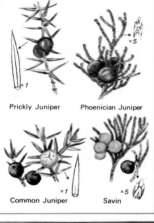

Prickly Juniper    Phoenician Juniper

Common Juniper    Savin

## Common Juniper
*Juniperus communis*

  *

Probably the most widely distributed woody plant of the northern hemisphere, occurring in many forms, on the tops of high mountains and in the lowlands, from the far north to the Mediterranean, from Canada to Japan. The sharp-pointed needles are in whorls of 3; they have a single pale band on the upper (inner) surface (p. 27 (1)), and are grey-green beneath. Male cones solitary (c), cylindrical,

b

c

26

usually on different bushes to the females. Female cones 6–9 mm, at first glaucous-green then bluish (2), finally black in the second year; usually 3-seeded. The Dwarf Juniper, ssp. *nana*, of mountains and the north, has smaller close-set, up-turned or in-curved, often blunt needles. It usually grows in spreading mats. Aromatic oils are obtained from the leaves and fruits.

Common Juniper

Prickly Juniper

## Prickly Juniper
*Juniperus oxycedrus*

  *

A shrub or small tree distinguished by its needle-leaves with two white bands on the upper surface (3), and its reddish to yellowish ripe cones, 7–15 mm (4). Needles variable, sharp-pointed or blunt. Often replaces Common Juniper along Mediterranean coastlands and dry hills, usually within 100 km of the sea.

## Syrian Juniper
*Juniperus drupacea*

The European juniper with the longest needle-leaves and largest fruit. A dense conical tree with whorls of 3, spiny-pointed leaves, 1–2.5 cm, with two conspicuous white bands above. Cones bloomed, brown or bluish-black, 2–2.5 cm. Bark orange-brown. Native of S. Greece.

# CYPRESS FAMILY

## Phoenician Juniper
### *Juniperus phoenicea*

A shrub or small tree with slender cord-like twigs covered with tiny triangular scale-leaves, in ranks of 4 or 6. Scale-leaves distinctive with a narrow papery border (p. 26). Ripe cones dark reddish, 8–14 mm. Native, mainly in dry hills, in the Mediterranean region.

## Savin
### *Juniperus sabina*

A low, often creeping, shrub with a strong disagreeable odour. Scale-leaves close-pressed to stem (1). Cones (2) 4–6 mm. Found in mountains of C. and S. Europe.
Similar is Spanish Juniper, *J. thurifera*, but it is an erect bluish-green tree of the mountains of Spain and France. Twigs quadrangular, scale-leaves free at tip (4), cones (3) 7–8 mm.

## Stinking Juniper
### *Juniperus foetidissima*

Distinguished by the irregularly arranged quadrangular twigs, 1 mm wide (not two-ranked). Scale-leaves free at the tips (p. 29 (2)); foliage very fetid when crushed. Cones 7–12 mm, reddish-brown to nearly black when ripe; seeds 1 or 2. Mountains of S. Balkans. Similar to and often confused with the following species.

## Grecian Juniper
*Juniperus excelsa*

A conical tree, later broad and spreading, native of the Balkan peninsula and widespread further east; found on dry rocky mountain slopes. Twigs rounded, two-ranked, very slender, less than 1 mm across, with ovate, acute, or blunt scale-leaves (1), with a glandular furrow on the back. Cones 8 mm, ripening in second year to dark purplish-brown; seeds 4–6.

## Pencil Cedar
*Juniperus virginiana*

  ‡

A conical tree, 30 m, with a straight, often buttressed trunk, with reddish bark peeling in narrow strips. Twigs very slender; scale-leaves and needle-leaves often present together. Cones violet-brown, 4–6 mm. The most widely distributed N. American conifer, sometimes planted for timber in S. and C. Europe.

## Alerce
*Tetraclinis articulata*

A rare, drought-resistant tree of N. Africa just extending to Malta and S. Spain. It has flattened spray-like branchlets with scale-leaves in four ranks. Woody cones unique in having only four scales, two blunt and two pointed. Known as Thyine wood in Biblical times and very valuable for cabinet-making and for its resin known as 'sandarac'.

×1    1    ×3

Grecian Juniper

×2½

×6   2     ×1

Stinking Juniper

a

b       c

×3

female flowers

cone

seed

scale

×1    ×1

## YEW FAMILY                                   Taxaceae

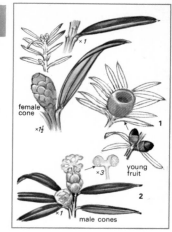

Distinguished from all other conifers by the male cones (2) which have flat-topped, peltate scales with the pollen sacs beneath. Also by the female 'cones' (1) which are one-seeded, becoming purplish and surrounded when ripe by a brightly coloured, fleshy scale or *aril*. A small family of 3 genera and 13 species; only one is native in Europe. The leaves are flattened and broadly needle-like, arranged in opposite pairs on side branches, and the foliage can be mistaken for that of redwoods, hemlocks and some firs, but their cones are quite different. The foliage is poisonous to cattle, particularly when withered. The seeds are poisonous to humans, but not the fleshy aril.

### Yew
*Taxus baccata*

   † *

A sombre dark green, broadly pyramidal tree or shrub, with ascending or spreading horizontal branches and dark reddish trunk. Leaves 1–3 cm, dark glossy green above, paler beneath. Widespread in woods and thickets in Europe, becoming rarer to the east. It is estimated that yews can live up to 2,000 years. There are many cultivated forms.

a

b

## WILLOW FAMILY                              Salicaceae

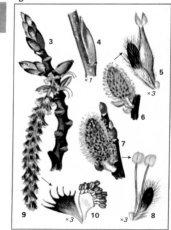

A family of deciduous trees and shrubs with one-sexed catkins occurring on different plants. Each catkin has a central axis bearing numerous tiny flowers, each flower in the axil of a papery bract. Male flowers (8), (10) with two or several stamens; female flowers (5) with a single ovary. Fruit dry, splitting into 2–4 valves (see p. 33) releasing numerous seeds with tufts of white hairs (see p. 33). The family comprises both willows and poplars. Willows are insect pollinated with stiff, nectar-bearing catkins (6), (7), and buds with a single scale (4). Poplars are wind pollinated with usually long pendulous catkins (9), and buds with several scales (3). Both willows and poplars hybridize freely making identification often difficult. A family of about 350 species; about 70 are European. Many willows are dwarf shrubs below 2 m.

**The WILLOWS** (*Salix*) (main groups)

| | | |
|---|---|---|
| Tree Willows. | Large trees. Leaves smooth, narrow-lanceolate, toothed. Catkins appearing with leaves; bracts pale. | **White** (p31), **Crack** (p32), **Weeping** (p32), **Almond-Leaved** (p33), **Bay-Leaved** (p33) |
| Sallows. | Shrubs, rarely trees. Leaves usually tough, wrinkled. Catkins appearing before leaves; bracts black-tipped. | **Sallow** (p33), **Grey Sallow** (p34), **Tea-Leaved** (p35), **Violet** (p35), *atrocinerea* (p34) |
| Osiers. | Shrubs with long pliant twigs. Leaves long, narrow. Catkins usually appearing before leaves. | **Osier** (p35), **Hoary** (p36), **Purple Osier** (p36). |

Tree Willow    Sallow    Osier

**White Willow** (a)
*Salix alba*
**Golden Willow** (b)
*S.* ssp. *vitellina*

🌿 ⬛ *

The former is a tall tree to 25 m with a stout trunk and spreading branches, but often pollarded. Twigs, buds, and leaves covered with silvery hairs, giving a very distinctive white sheen to the foliage. Leaves long-pointed, finely-toothed, hairy on both surfaces, especially below, or nearly hairless above; leaf stalk without glands. Twigs do not break off easily. Catkins appear with young leaves; stamens 2. It is often planted for its pliant young twigs used for basketry, and for its timber which is light and tough.
The latter has bright orange or yellow young twigs and dark green leaves.
Cricket-bat Willow, ssp. *coerulea*, has dull greenish-blue leaves, purple twigs, and a tapering pyramidal silhouette.

a

b

White Willow

# WILLOW FAMILY

## Crack Willow
*Salix fragilis*

 ■ † *

So called because the twigs readily break off with a snap at the
base (1). A large tree to 25 m,
similar to the White Willow but
differing from it in having larger,
glossy leaves, glaucous and
waxy beneath and with glands
(3). Twigs and buds (2) becoming hairless, shining, often reddish; buds duckbill-shaped. Catkins slender, cylindrical, pointed, appearing with the leaves.
Capsule stalked. Coral-like, sub-
merged roots are pink, not white
as in White Willow. The fact
that twigs break off easily and
root, enables the tree to spread
rapidly downstream. A widespread European tree. Hybrids
between it and White Willow
are probably the commonest and
the most widely distributed of
willow hybrids.

a

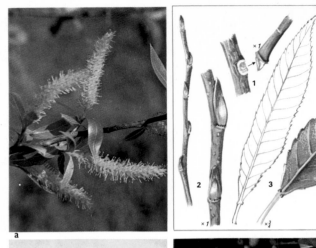

b

c

## Weeping Willows
*Salix × chrysocoma*

 ■

Distinguished by their long, pendulous twigs falling almost to
the ground. Leaves hairless at
maturity. Widely grown for
ornament; most commonly
planted is × *chrysocoma* (hybrid
with Golden Willow) which has
yellow pendulous twigs and
leaves with silky hairs.
*S. babylonica* has brown twigs.

d

e

## Almond-Leaved or French Willow
*Salix triandra*

Distinguished by its flaky bark and slender male catkins which have 3 stamens in each flower (1). Leaves shining, often glaucous beneath, and stipules (2) persistent. A shrub or small tree with greenish or reddish-brown twigs.
A hybrid with Osier, × *mollissima*, is often grown in N.–W. Europe for basket-making.

## Bay-Leaved Willow
*Salix pentandra*

A shrub or small tree of moorlands and bogs throughout Europe. Its elliptical, shining green, sticky, fragrant young leaves are unmistakable. Twigs shining, hairless, deep brown, with pale outstanding buds. Catkins appearing late in the season amongst the leaves; stamens usually 5.

## Sallow, Goat Willow
*Salix caprea*

 †

A shrub or small tree widely distributed in damp woods and coppices in Europe. The leaves (3) are broader than those of most willows; they are variable but often broadly ovate, dark green above and densely grey-woolly beneath, and rather leathery and wrinkled. Margin toothed or entire; veins prominent beneath; stipules usually large. Young twigs grey-haired; winter twigs (4) shiny, hairless;

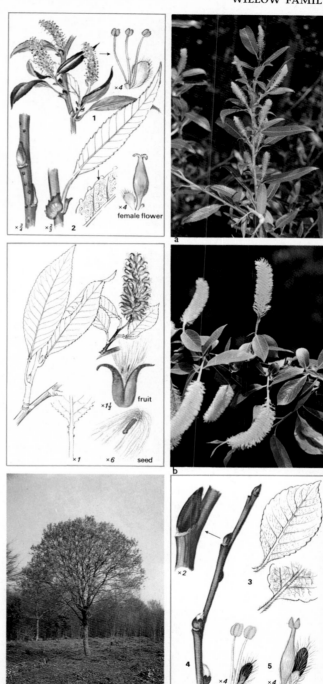

×4

1

×¾   ×⅔   2

×4   female flower

a

×1½   fruit

×1   ×6   seed

b

c

×2   3

4   5

×4   ×4

33

buds reddish, tips not pressed to stem. Bark grey and smooth at first, then widely fissured and pale brown. Catkins conspicuous on bare twigs—females green (b), males yellow (a); bracts black-tipped (p. 33 (5)). Sallows hybridize freely. A number of sallows grow to over 2 m, but their identification requires considerable experience; they are not described here.

### Grey Sallow
*Salix cinerea*

A shrub to 6 m of damp woods, marshes, and fens throughout most of Europe. Distinguished from Sallow by its winter twigs which remain velvety-hairy; its narrower leaves; and its twigs which, when stripped of bark, are finely ridged. Leaves lanceolate to oblanceolate (1), rounded or narrowly pointed at apex, densely grey-hairy beneath; stipules persistent. Male catkins yellow (2), female catkins green (3), both ovoid 2.5–5 cm.
Very similar is *S. atrocinerea*, a shrub of W. Europe, identified by the presence of some rust-coloured hairs on the undersides of the leaves. Winter twigs reddish, hairless, or thinly hairy. Often found in drier places than Grey Willows; the two species hybridize frequently. Note: drawings and photographs are of *S. atrocinerea*.

## Tea-Leaved Willow
*Salix phylicifolia*

A shrub to 4 m with dark, shining twigs and rather small ovate to narrowly elliptic pointed leaves, which are shining green above, and glaucous beneath. Catkins flowering with the young leaves. One of a group of willows very difficult to identify, as they hybridize freely with other groups. Native in the N. and the mountains of C. Europe.

## Violet Willow
*Salix daphnoides*

Distinguished by its beautiful, bluish-purple bloomed young winter twigs, and its showy, silvery-white male catkins, which appear early in the year. Leaves with glandular teeth, dark shining green above, glaucous beneath. A shrub or small tree to 10 m, native of Scandinavia, widely planted in C. and E. Europe.

## Common Osier
*Salix viminalis*

  *

Its long, narrow leaves which are dark green above and glistening silky-haired beneath are unmistakable. Leaf blade about 1.5 cm wide, with inrolled margins. Twigs long, straight, flexible, felted when young. A shrub of C. and W. Europe; often planted for its twigs which are cut annually from stools and used for basketry.

female

female catkins male catkins

female male

35

# WILLOW FAMILY

## Hoary Willow
### *Salix elaeagnos*

The willow with the most delicate and slender leaves of all.
Like the Osier it has leaves with
felty hairs and inrolled margins
beneath; young twigs grey and
hairy. Catkins long, narrow, and
curved, appearing with young
leaves. River beds and banks of
C. Europe.

## Purple Osier
### *Salix purpurea*

A rather slender shrub with
shining, usually purplish, young
twigs, and narrow, waxy, bluish-
green, hairless leaves which are
often opposite, particularly at
the ends of twigs. Male catkins
attractive, with black bracts, silvery hairs, and red anthers; 
stamens fused and appearing as
one. Native to C. and S. Europe;
planted for basketry. Frequently
hybridizes with Osier.

## THE POPLARS                    POPULUS

Easily distinguished from the willows by their broad-bladed
leaves which tremble in the wind. Botanically distinguished by
their winter buds which have several outer scales (1), and the
bracts (2) (3) of the flowers which are toothed or comb-like.
(Buds of willows have 1 scale; willow bracts are entire.) Like
willows, poplars hybridize freely, and many hybrid forms,
particularly between Black Poplar and Cottonwood, are cultivated. These often grow more vigorously and produce heavier
crops of timber than the wild parents. Both poplars and willows
grow in damp places, where water lies near the surface but
poplars favour better drained soils which are only periodically
flooded.

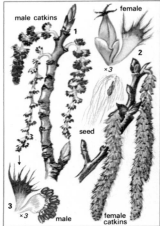

**Key to POPLARS** (*Populus*)

1 Leaves on long shoots densely woolly beneath. — **White** (p37), **Grey** (p38)

1 Leaves on long shoots not densely woolly beneath.

  2 Leaves without a narrow translucent margin.

    3 Leaf stalk flattened from side to side. — **Aspen** (p38)

    3 Leaf stalk rounded in section. — **Balsam** (p40), *simonii* (p41)

  2 Leaves with a narrow translucent margin (1).

    4 Leaves without ciliate margin; trunk with bosses. — **Black** (p39), **Lombardy** (p39), **Berlin** (p39)

    4 Leaves with a minutely ciliate margin (see p. 39 (4)); trunk without bosses. — **Cottonwood** (p40), **Hybrid Black** (p40), **Italian** (p40)

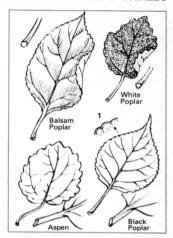

## White Poplar, Abele
*Populus alba*

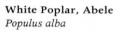

A tall, usually somewhat leaning tree to 30 m, with pale greyish-white crown and leaves which are pure white beneath. Upper unfolding leaves (2) 3–5-lobed, at first white on both sides, then dark shining green above. Lower leaves (4) ovate and shallowly lobed, with flattened leaf stalks; sucker leaves deeply lobed. Young buds and twigs white, cottony, becoming pale brown (3). Bark at first white or greyish, covered with diamond-shaped lenticels, later black and rugged. Male catkins appear before the leaves, large, crimson, softly hairy. Female catkins greenish-yellow. Native of most of Europe, but often planted for timber, as shelter near the sea, and for ornament. Poplars are very quick-growing and can produce useful timber in 30 years, but the wood is light and porous.

a

b

c

# WILLOW FAMILY

## Grey Poplar
*Populus canescens*

Similar to the White Poplar but a more attractive tree with undersides of leaves and twigs covered with dense greyish hairs. Upper leaves (2) with wide irregular teeth, not lobed, soon becoming hairless and glossy above. Leaves on short shoots, rounded like Aspen. Bracts of flowers (1) cut into slender tapering teeth (teeth broad and shallow in White Poplar). A large tree to 35 m, upper trunk silvery-grey with lines of diamond-shaped lenticels, and lower trunk dark brown to blackish, strongly ridged. A suckering tree of damp woods and watersides throughout much of S., C. and W. Europe. Often planted for ornament and for shelter near the sea.

## Aspen
*Populus tremula*

  † *

The most widely distributed European poplar, distinguished from all others by the almost rounded to oval, wavy-margined leaves (p. 39 (2)). Leaf stalks flattened from side to side allowing a quivering movement of the leaf blade. Leaves of sucker shoots (p. 39 (1)) triangular-heart-shaped, and greyish-hairy; upper leaves soon hairless. Bark smooth, pale grey on young trunks and upper bole, becom-

ing dark grey and rough on old trunks. Buds resinous, plump, and pointed. Male catkins purplish-grey and very silky when young (p. 38d). Female catkins green, silky-haired. Found from the Arctic circle to the edge of alpine glaciers; it commonly grows on mountain screes, banks and river gravels where it suckers freely and helps to consolidate the soil.

## Black Poplars
*Populus nigra*

The true Black Poplar can be distinguished by the conspicuous rounded bosses on its trunk. It grows into a tall well-proportioned tree to 30 m, with short trunk and widely ascending branches forming a broad crown. Leaves diamond-shaped to oval, long-pointed, margin saw-toothed and with a translucent border (3), not ciliate and without glands at the base. Bark pale brown and more rugged than most. Fruiting catkins (b) 10–15 cm; bracts hairless, thus young catkins do not appear fluffy. Lombardy Poplar, *Italica,* has a very distinctive, slender, spire-like form (d). Other slender trees include the Berlin Poplar, × *berolinensis*; distinguished by the rounded not flattened leaf-stalks. Many hybrid forms of Black Poplar and Cottonwood, known as × *canadensis* (p. 40a), have been selected and are grown in C. and S. Europe for timber. Two commonly planted forms are Black Italian Poplar, *Serotina* (p. 40b), with

female catkin

1
2
3
4
Black Poplar
Hybrid Black Poplar
Black Italian Poplar

bronze young foliage and hairless yellowish-buff twigs. It is male only. Hybrid Black Poplar, *Regenerata,* with pale brown young foliage appearing earlier than the preceding. Its buds turn outwards (p. 39 (4)), the leaf margins are ciliate like *Serotina.*

a

b

### Cottonwood, American Black Poplar
*Populus deltoides*

  ‡

An American tree, a parent of the many cultivated hybrids now so widely planted for timber in Europe. Distinguished by its large, oval-triangular leaf blades, 10–18 cm, which have a densely ciliate margin, and glands at the base of the blade. Twigs often strongly angled. Stamens 30–60 in each flower. Planted for timber and along roadsides in C. Europe.

c

d

### Balsam Poplar, Balm of Gilead
*Populus gileadensis*

  ‡

A very fast growing tree with sticky buds, which particularly in spring has a strong pungent aroma of balsam. Leaves golden-green, triangular-ovate-pointed, with translucent ciliate margin, densely hairy on the veins beneath. Twigs stout, angled. Readily suckering. Planted for timber and occasionally naturalized.

e

Cottonwood

Balsam Poplar

*Populus simonii*

  ‡

A native of N. China, occasionally planted for timber in C.
Europe. A small, handsome,
narrow-crowned tree with
slender, pendulous branches
and bright green leaves. Branches reddish-brown, hairless;
leaves small, 4–12 cm, diamond-
shaped, hairless; leaf stalk
short, rounded.

a

b

# WALNUT FAMILY      Juglandaceae

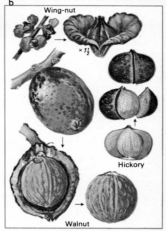

A family of about 60 deciduous trees with large pinnate leaves.
Catkins one-sexed; males pendulous with numerous tiny flowers
composed of several bracts and 3–40 stamens; females in a
stalkless cluster of 2–3 ovaries with large fleshy stigmas. Fruit a
somewhat fleshy drupe, or a nut. Three genera, walnuts, hickories and wing-nuts are planted in Europe, only the Common
Walnut is native. Walnuts are distinguished by their solitary
catkins; pith of twigs discontinuous with cross partitions;
aromatic leaves; and large fruits. Hickories have male catkins
in clusters of three or more; pith continuous; non-aromatic
leaves; and fruits splitting. Wing-nuts have winged fruits;
buds without bud scales; non-aromatic leaves; and pith with
cross partitions.

**Common Walnut**
*Juglans regia*

  † *

A native tree of mountain
woods in the Balkan peninsula
which has been cultivated and
become naturalized for so long
in other parts of Europe that its
real distribution is obscure.
A magnificent tree to 30 m,
with a broad crown and lustrous clear green foliage, and
silvery-grey bark which becomes deeply fissured with age.
Leaves with 7–9 large obovate

c

d

41

leaflets, each 6–15 cm long, hairless, very fragrant when crushed. Fruit large, globular, 4–5 cm; the outer green fleshy part turns black and decays revealing the deeply wrinkled nutshell. Within lies the contorted nut—a delicious and important food. The timber is of high quality, beautifully marked, strong and durable and much in demand.

a

## Black Walnut
*Juglans nigra*

  ‡

A N. American tree distinguished by its dark brownish, deeply fissured bark and its large pinnate leaves. Leaflets 15–23, oval long-pointed, irregularly toothed, hairy and glandular beneath, 6–12 cm long. Fruit 3.5–5 cm, hairy; stone strongly ridged, not splitting. Extensively planted for timber in parts of C. and E. Europe.

b

c

## Bitternut Hickory (d)
*Carya cordiformis*
## Shellbark Hickory (e)
*Carya laciniosa*

  ‡

These two species of hickory and several others from N. America are sometimes planted for timber in C. Europe. Distinguished by their pinnate leaves, male catkins in branches of three or more and their small rounded fruits with dry husks which at length split releasing the nut (p. 41).

d

e

## Caucasian Wing-Nut
*Pterocarya fraxinifolia*

  ‡

A native tree of the Caucasus and Iran, sometimes planted in Europe for timber in damp places. It has large pinnate leaves with 11–20 pairs of sharp-toothed overlapping leaflets. Fruiting catkins un-mistakable, long, pendulous, green, bearing numerous winged nuts (p. 41). Trunk dull grey; buds naked; tree freely sucker-ing and forming thickets.

a

b

# BIRCH FAMILY                    Betulaceae

Deciduous trees and shrubs with both male and female catkins on the same tree, often flowering before the leaves. Male cat-kins pendulous with numerous minute flowers in threes sur-rounded by bracts. Female catkins erect. Fruiting catkins dense, in cylindrical, usually pendulous, cone-like clusters; fruit winged. A small family of about 70 species, mostly of the N. hemisphere; 6 species over 2 m high are native in Europe, in two genera. Birches have usually pale, stripping bark, and fragmenting female catkins, with 3-lobed bracts. Alders have dark bark, and woody cone-like female catkins which do not fragment.

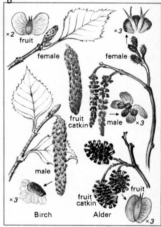

## Silver Birch
*Betula pendula*

   † *

A graceful tree to 30 m, found in most of Europe, with white bark and usually long, slender, pendulous twigs. Distinguished by the coarse double-toothed leaf margins (1), the hairless twigs which are often rough with resinous secretions (3) and the hairless fruit. Winter buds sticky, conical (3). Female catkins at first slender and erect, later pendulous (2), finally shedding the winged fruit and

c

43

## BIRCH FAMILY

the distinctive 3-lobed 'fleur-de-
luc' bracts. Male catkins (b)
pendulous, appearing with
young leaves. A short-lived
tree, often a pioneer and rapidly
colonizing sandy, peaty, acid
soils by means of its winged
seeds. Intolerant to shade and
eventually smothered by larger,
more long-lived trees such as
oaks or pines. Often planted
as a nurse in forestry plantations.

### Hairy Birch
*Betula pubescens*

Very like the former, often
hybridizing with it, but distinguished by the single set of
teeth on its leaf margin (1), its
usually hairy young twigs
without resin-glands (2), and
its minutely hairy fruits. A
smaller, very variable, more
upright tree than Silver Birch,
to 20 m, with spreading branches and greyish or brownish
bark. Found on poor acid soils
in N. and C. Europe.

### Common Alder
*Alnus glutinosa*

  † *

A small pyramidal tree to 20 m
or more, or a coppiced shrub,
growing by the water's edge or
in swamps, distinguished at any
time of year by the clusters
of small dark, ovoid 'cones'
(p. 45(1)). In spring the reddish-
yellow pendulous male catkins,
topped by a cluster of tiny
reddish female 'cones' appear
on bare twigs together with the
previous year's 'cones'. The

44

short-stalked buds and young sticky twigs are characteristic. Leaves hairless, with a notched apex and wedge-shaped base, with a double-toothed margin. Bark dark brown, fissured. Found throughout Europe, except the extreme north and south. The timber is soft but durable under water; the bark is rich in tannins. A valuable tree for conserving banks of rivers and lakes.

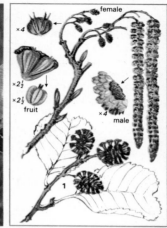

a

## Grey Alder
*Alnus incana*

Widely dispersed in Europe but not native in Britain. Distinguished by the silvery-grey hairs on the undersides of the leaves and young shoots and by its acute-pointed, boldly toothed leaves, with 7–12 pairs of side-veins (5–8 in Common Alder). Buds not sticky. Fruiting 'cones' 11–17 mm, ovoid to rounded. Bark smooth, grey or yellowish. A small waterside tree or shrub, usually not more than 10 m, most commonly found on flood plains and mountain valleys where it suckers freely. Often planted to help consolidate the soil in flood control, to stabilize glacier moraines, mine tips, etc. This and the previous species hybridize where they occur together.

b

c

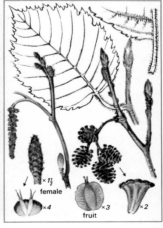

# BIRCH FAMILY

## Smooth Alder
### *Alnus rugosa (serrulata)*

  ‡

A N. American shrub or small tree frequently planted and naturalized in C. Europe. Distinguished by its leaves which have a finely and regularly toothed margin, and reddish-brown hairs on the undersides (1), at least in the axils of the veins. Young twigs reddish-brown, at first hairy and sticky. 'Cones' 4–10 in a cluster.

## Italian Alder
### *Alnus cordata*

A handsome pyridamal tree to 15 m with smooth, unfurrowed bark and the largest 'cones' (1.5–3 cm) of any alder, in clusters of 1–4. Leaves glossy deep green, paler beneath, rounded heart-shaped, finely toothed, hairless or with tufts of hairs in the axils of veins. Buds and twigs sticky. A native of damp thickets in S. Italy and Corsica.

## Green Alder
### *Alnus viridis*

  †

Usually a small bush to about 2.5 m forming thickets in the mountains of C. and S.–E. Europe. Unlike other alders in having the catkins flowering as the leaves appear, and having stalkless buds (2). Twigs hairless; leaves variable, blunt or long-pointed, hairless or hairy beneath, sticky when young. Fruiting 'cones' in clusters of 3–5.

46

# HAZEL FAMILY                    Corylaceae

A small family of about 50 species of catkin-bearing, deciduous trees and shrubs with nuts which are enclosed, or partly surrounded, by a papery greenish bract, or *involucre*; 6 are native in Europe. Male catkins (1) pendulous, with one minute flower in each bract. Female flowers paired in the axil of each bract. The 3 European genera are distinguished by their fruit, otherwise they are often very similar in appearance. Hazel has a cluster of large nuts, each partly surrounded by a leafy, toothed bract. Hornbeam has a catkin of small nuts (b) each with a much longer three-lobed or toothed bract (2). Hop-Hornbeam has hop-like catkins of small nuts each enclosed in a baggy envelope (3).

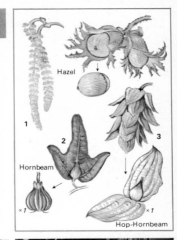

## Hornbeam
*Carpinus betulus*

   † *

A widely distributed European tree with a characteristically smooth grey, fluted trunk. It grows to 25 m and has a rounded crown with ascending branches and ultimately pendulous branchlets, but it is often coppiced or pollarded resulting in numerous branches arising from the stool or trunk. Distinguished in fruit by its unique hanging clusters (b), 5–15 cm long, of large, three-lobed leafy bracts each with a small, hard, ridged nut (4). Twigs, leaves, and bark can be mistaken for those of Beech, but Hornbeam buds (5) are shorter, broader, and pressed to the stem; leaves double-toothed. The timber is very hard-wearing and tough. A handsome tree which colours well in autumn and makes good hedges.

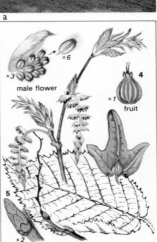

47

# HAZEL FAMILY

## Oriental Hornbeam
*Carpinus orientalis*

A shrub or small tree of the hills of the Balkan peninsula, spreading as far west as Italy and Sicily. Distinguished most readily from Hornbeam by the smaller fruit clusters, 3–5 cm long, which have dark green irregularly toothed triangular-oval bracts about 2 cm long, not three-lobed. Leaves smaller, 2.5–6 cm, double-toothed.

## Hop-Hornbeam
*Ostrya carpinifolia*

  †

A slender-branched, medium sized, deciduous tree, easily recognized in fruit (3). Fruiting catkins ovoid, pendulous, very similar in size and appearance to those of Hop—hence its common name. Individual nuts enclosed in papery bag-like involucre (2). In spring the clusters of very long, plump male catkins shed their pollen as the leaves break; the females are inconspicuous, terminal, and erect. Leaves, recalling Hornbeam, double-toothed but teeth sharper and blades hairy above when young, unlike Hornbeam. Twigs hairy; buds spindle-shaped (1). Trunk brown, longitudinally fissured. Native of S. Europe, from France eastwards, in bushy places mainly on coastal hills and mountains inland.

a

b

c

d

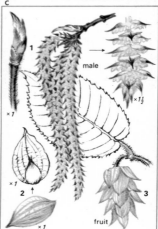

## Hazel
### *Corylus avellana*

  † *

A well-known, widely distributed, large deciduous shrub to
6 m of woods and thickets
throughout Europe. Its clusters
of brown nuts, each encircled
by deeply lacerated green
bracts, about as long as the nut,
are unmistakable. Leaves rounded, long-pointed, margin
double-toothed, often shallowly
lobed; leaf stalk with glandular
hairs. Twigs densely covered
with stiff reddish glandular
hairs; buds blunt. Male catkins
appearing in autumn, round and
plump, not elongating and
shedding pollen till the first
mild days of the new year.
Female catkins (1) appearing
in spring, bud-like, with
crimson stigmas. Usually a
spreading shrub, but often
coppiced for its pliant branches
used in hurdle-making. The
nuts are edible and nutritious.

## Turkish Hazel (d)
### *Corylus colurna*
## Filbert (e)
### *Corylus maxima*

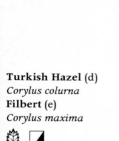

Two trees or shrubs, native of
the Balkans, have bracts much
longer than the nuts. Turkish
Hazel has bracts cut into long
narrow toothed lobes, and long-
pointed stipules. Filbert has a
tubular bract, constricted above
the nut with toothed margin.
The latter is widely cultivated
for its edible nuts.

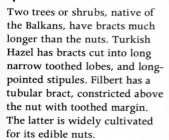

# BEECH FAMILY                    Fagaceae

Oak

Beech

Sweet Chestnut

A very important family of deciduous and evergreen trees which are the dominant forest-formers of the summer deciduous forests of the temperate regions of the world. Forests of oak and beech covered much of Central Europe before the advent of man. These catkin bearing trees are recognized by their characteristic fruit—a nut surrounded by, or enveloped in, an involucre of fused bracts. There are three European genera. Beech and chestnut have several nuts enclosed in a tough, splitting, involucre covered with spines. Oaks have a 'cup' of fused scales encircling the base of each nut. A family of about 600 species; about 27, mainly oaks, are native in Europe.

## Beech
*Fagus sylvatica*

   † *

A quite unmistakable large tree to 30 m, with smooth metallic-grey trunk, glossy leaves, spindle-shaped buds, and triangular-sectioned nuts. A dominant forest tree, often forming pure forests, under which few plants can grow, on light soils in the lowlands, and on mountain slopes in a zone below the coniferous forest zone. It is native from Spain to Greece and reaches S. Scandinavia. Leaves ovate, silky-haired, with 5–8 pairs of lateral veins. Catkins appearing with the leaves (3), the males numerous, pendulous; the females (1) inconspicuous. The woody fruits (2), or 'mast' are covered with slender-pointed spines, and split into 4 valves when ripe; the nuts are edible. The bronze autumn colouring and delicate pale green spring foliage help to confirm it as one of the most beautiful of European trees.

a

b

c

## Oriental Beech
*Fagus orientalis*

It replaces the Common Beech in
the mountains of E. Greece,
Rumania, and Bulgaria. Very
similar but distinguished by the
broader, larger leaves, 9–12 cm,
with 8–12 pairs of side-veins.
Spines on the fruit blunt, linear-
oblong, the lower spines spoon-
shaped. Trees with intermediate
characters are found in C. and
W. Balkans.

## Sweet Chestnut
*Castanea sativa*

   † *

A massive tree to 30 m with
longitudinally fissured, often
characteristically spirally-twist-
ed bark, large saw-toothed
leaves, and spiny fruits. It is a
native of S.–E. Europe but it
has been extensively planted
elsewhere—probably brought
to Britain by the Romans—for
its delicious, edible nuts. The
large, glossy leaves, 10–25 cm,
with conspicuous side veins and
bristly teeth are easily recognized. It is unique in having the
catkins flowering late in the
summer long after the leaves are
mature. They are insect pollinated, erect and spike-like with
male clusters (1) towards the tip
and a few female flowers at the
base (2). The glossy nuts are
set free when the outer spiny
cup splits open. The timber is
strong and durable and is used
mostly for outdoor work.

## BEECH FAMILY

**Keys to OAKS** (*Quercus*)

1 Leaves evergreen and leathery (1) or half-evergreen (2) and remaining on tree over winter. **Kermes** (p54), **Cork** (p53), **Holm** (p52), **Round-Leaved** (p53), **Algerian** (p59), **Portuguese** (p59) (*see also* **Macedonian, Valonia**)

1 Leaves deciduous, falling in autumn.

  2 Fruit ripening in second year and situated on leafless part of twigs (6).

    3 Cup scales spreading or reflexed (3). **Macedonian** (p55), **Valonia** (p55), **Turkey** (p55)

    3 Cup scales pressed to cup (4). **Red** (p56), **Pin** (p56)

  2 Fruit ripening in first year, situated on present year's twigs among leaves (5) (7).

    4 Fruit long-stalked (5); cup scales fused. **Common** (p57), *pedunculiflora* (p57)

    4 Fruit stalkless or very short-stalked (7); cup scales not fused.

      5 Young twigs woolly-haired; leaf stalk not grooved. **Hungarian** (p59), **Pyrenean** (p59), **White** (p58), *virgiliana* (p60)

      5 Young twigs hairless or glossy silky-haired; leaf grooved. **Durmast** (p57), *polycarpa* (p58), *dalechampii* (p58)

In addition there are the following local species: *Q. brachyphylla*, Greece, Crete; *Q. congesta*, France, Sicily, Sardinia; *Q. fruticosa*, Portugal, Spain; *Q. hartwissiana*, Bulgaria, Turkey; *Q. infectoria*, N. Greece, Turkey; *Q. mas*, France, Spain; *Q. sicula*, Sicily.

## Holm Oak
*Quercus ilex*

 † *

The most widely distributed of European evergreen oaks, an indicator of a typically Mediterranean climate, with hot dry summers and autumn to spring rains. Often planted for ornament, however, and shelter further north. Distinguished by its adult leaves (8) which have grey felted hairs on the undersides, and its grey-felted young twigs. Leaves of sucker shoots (10) prickly, holly-like, green

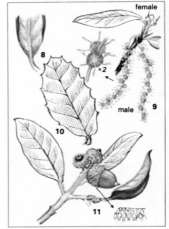

beneath. Catkins (p. 52 (9))
occurring with the new, often
reddish young leaves in late
spring. The fruit ripens during
the first year; acorn cup with
adpressed grey-haired scales
(p. 52 (11)). If left undisturbed
by man it can form dense low
forests casting heavy shade, but
it is often encountered as a low
bush. The timber is hard and
dense.

## Round-Leaved Oak
*Quercus rotundifolia*

A small rounded evergreen tree
of dry evergreen thickets in S.–
W. Europe, closely related to
Holm Oak and often treated as a
sub-species, but leaves more
rounded, usually broadly ovate
to rounded, with 5–8 pairs of
side veins, greyish-glaucous
above. Stipules thin, papery,
nearly hairless. Nuts sweet,
whereas Holm Oak nuts are
bitter.

## Cork Oak
*Quercus suber*

  † *

This tree produces the cork of
commerce; it is conspicuous in
its native Mediterranean home
with its very rugged, extremely
thick, spongy, whitish bark.
The small, shiny, evergreen
leaves which are grey-haired beneath, are difficult to distinguish
from the Holm Oak but they
have a rather curved, sinuous
mid-vein (2), also the upper
scales of the mature acorn cup
are slightly spreading (1), not

adpressed to the cup. Most cork oak woods are semi-natural and maintained by man in open stands with the scrub kept in check, or cleared. Portugal and S.–W. Spain are the main cork-producing areas but the tree grows as far east as W. Yugoslavia. The bark is stripped from the trunk every 8–10 years, revealing the pinkish under-bark which soon darkens.

### Kermes or Holly Oak
*Quercus coccifera*

 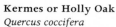

A widely distributed Mediterranean evergreen oak, usually encountered as a low impenetrable holly-like bush often intensively grazed (c), scattered over large tracts of the hottest and dryest hillsides. Leaves small, 1.5–4 cm, stiff, shining dark green with very prickly spines on the margin, quite hairless beneath when mature (2). New leaves (1) appearing with the catkins in spring are often bronzed and hairy. The fruit ripens in the second year amongst the older leaves. Acorn cup (3) with rigid, spiny, spreading scales. If left undisturbed, Holly Oak can grow into a small tree (d), but trees are only occasionally seen in the wild.

## Macedonian Oak
### *Quercus trojana (macedonica)*

A distinctive oak of the Balkan peninsula and S.–E. Italy with small, oblong, shiny leaves with 16–24 coarse, bristly, marginal teeth (2). Densely branched, small or medium-sized tree, deciduous or semi-evergreen; twigs grey and scurfy. Fruit ripening in second year; acorn cup with lowest scales adpressed, the middle scales reflexed, and the upper ones up-curved (1).

## Valonia Oak
### *Quercus macrolepis (aegilops)*

   *

Well known for its very large acorn cups, used for tanning, ink-making, and dyeing. A small, semi-evergreen tree of the S. Balkans and S.–E. Italy. Leaves with 3–7 pairs of triangular, bristly-tipped lobes (3), sometimes double-lobed, densely woolly beneath, smooth above. Acorn cup (4) up to 5 cm across, with spreading scales.

## Turkey Oak
### *Quercus cerris*

  †

A large, sombre, deciduous tree to 35 m, distinguished from all other European oaks by the long narrow stipules (5) round the buds and at the base of the leaves. Leaves dull, becoming shiny, rough-textured above, with woolly, grey-brown hairs beneath, and usually with 10–14 narrow pointed lobes or large teeth, but lobing very variable, particularly on sprout shoots. Male catkins (p. 56a) numerous.

Macedonian Oak

Valonia Oak

×2 female

male
×2

×1

5

6

Acorns clustered, very short-stalked, borne on last year's shoots (b) below the present year's leaves. Acorn cups (p. 55 (6)) 'mossy', densely covered with soft, pointed scales. Native tree of S.–C. Europe, from France to Turkey, but naturalized elsewhere as in Britain where it is the fastest growing oak. Its timber is of little value.

## Red Oak
*Quercus rubra (borealis)*

A N. American tree, often planted for timber and shelter in C. Europe; well-known for its often rich red autumn colouring. Leaves large, cut to half-way or less to mid-vein into 7–11 angular lobes, each with 1–3 bristly teeth; young twigs hairless, warted, red. Acorns squat, ripening during second year and the cup is shallow (1).

## Pin Oak
*Quercus palustris*

A native of N. America, now infrequently planted for timber mainly in E.–C. Europe. In general like the previous species but distinguished by its narrower leaves, lobed to more than half-way to mid-vein. Terminal branches slender, pendulous; buds tiny, 3 mm. Acorn cups small, 1–1.5 cm across (2). Autumn colouring even more brilliant than Red Oak.

## Common or Pedunculate Oak
*Quercus robur*

  *

The most widespread of the
European oaks, famous for its
dark brown, heavy, well-mark-
ed, extremely tough and durable
timber much in demand for
furniture making, and for
ship-building in the past. The
dominant forest-forming tree on
many of the deeper clay and
loam soils of C. Europe. In the
open it has a domed crown with
wide-spreading branches, but as
a forest tree it may grow to 45 m
with a tall straight trunk and
a narrow crown. Distinguished
by its long-stalked acorns (2);
its leaf blades with ear-like flaps
(1) where they meet the leaf
stalk, and the absence of hairs
on the underside of its mature
leaves.

*Q. pedunculiflora* of S.–E. Europe
differs in having leaves with persistent yellow-grey, woolly hairs
beneath. Scales of acorn cups
with a warty swelling and yellowish hairs.

## Durmast or Sessile Oak
*Quercus petraea*

  †

Very like the Common Oak and
often hybridizing with it, making some individual trees difficult to determine. Durmast Oak
is a forest-forming tree found in
much of Europe, particularly on
poorer, lighter, acid soils. It usually has a more open crown than
Common Oak, with straighter,
spreading branches. Botanically
distinguished by its leaves which
have a wedge-shaped base (p. 58
(2)), longer leaf stalk 1.5–2.5 cm,

and tufts of brownish hairs in the axils of the veins beneath. Fruits in stalkless clusters of 2–6, or stalk up to 1 cm. The timber is similar to that of Common Oak.

*Q. dalechampii* of S.–E. Europe is distinguished by its greyish, nearly hairless acorn cups which have scales with a conspicuous wart-like swelling (3); and mature leaves which are hairless beneath (1).

a

### White or Downy Oak
*Quercus pubescens (lanuginosa)*

  †

*Quercus polycarpa* (d)

The former is a widely distributed small tree or shrub of S. and C. Europe growing on dry, usually limestone slopes. Distinguished by its relatively small, shallow-lobed leaves (b) which are densely velvety-haired beneath, but become nearly hairless with age. Leaf stalk 2–12 mm. Twigs and buds densely grey-haired. Scales of acorn cups grey-woolly, closely adpressed.

The latter from S.–E. Europe is distinguished by its brown-haired acorn cup, with strongly swollen scales. Leaves rather leathery, 6–10 cm, with 7–10 pairs of shallow blunt lobes; leaf stalk 1.5–3.5 cm. Twigs, buds, and mature leaves hairless.

b

c

d

### Algerian Oak (a)
*Quercus canariensis*
### Portuguese Oak (b)
*Quercus faginea*

The former has large, boldly lobed, semi-evergreen leaves 6–18 cm, which are glaucous beneath. Young twigs and leaves with tufts of easily rubbed-off hairs. Scales of cup unequal, lower broader swollen, upper small. Tree to 30 m.
The latter, also semi-evergreen, is woolly-haired beneath. Cup scales velvety, swollen.

### Pyrenean Oak
*Quercus pyrenaica (toza)*

A deciduous tree to 20 m of the Iberian peninsula, France, and N. Italy. Leaves densely white-woolly beneath, soon more or less hairless above, deeply cut with 4–8 pairs of narrow acute lobes. Twigs woolly and pendulous. Fruit short stalked, scales of cup narrow lanceolate, blunt, loosely overlapping.

### Hungarian Oak
*Quercus frainetto (conferta)*

A large tree to 30 m with woolly-haired young twigs, large buds with persistent stipules, and large, very deeply and boldly lobed leaves 10–20 cm (p. 60 (b)). Leaf-blade with 7–9 pairs of lobes, often further lobed, hairy beneath, with ear-like flaps, where it meets the very short leaf stalk. Scales of acorn cup oblong-blunt, hairy, loosely overlapping. Native of woods and thickets in Balkans and Italy.

Hungarian Oak

Portuguese Oak

Q. virgiliana

Pyrenean Oak

Algerian Oak

*Q. virgiliana* is also from S. Europe, from Corsica eastwards. It has broadly obovate leaves with 5–7 pairs of wide usually lobed segments, and leaf stalk 1.5–2.5 cm. Cup scales ovate-lanceolate, loosely adpressed, with an erect point.

a

b

## ELM FAMILY · Ulmaceae

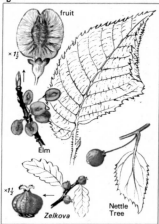

A family of about 150 species of temperate and tropical regions. 3 genera, the elms, nettle trees and *Zelkova*, comprising 9 species, are native to Europe. They are deciduous trees and shrubs with undivided, usually asymmetrical, lop-sided leaves. Flowers often clustered, small and inconspicuous, one-sexed, or hermaphrodite, appearing with or before the leaves. Flowers wind pollinated, with many stamens and an ovary with two feathery styles. Fruit a broadly winged nut in elms, a fleshy drupe in nettle trees, or an unwinged nut in *Zelkova*. Members of the family rarely form forests and have few economic uses except to supply coarse timber.

### Wych Elm
*Ulmus glabra*

 ■ *

A lofty tree to 40 m distinguished by the spreading, arching branches which arise low down on the main trunk, and by the absence of suckers. Leaves large, rounded to broadly obovate, the roughest in texture on the upper surface of all the elms, softly hairy beneath. Leaf margin double-toothed, and leaf base of the longer side forming a rounded lobe almost concealing the short leaf stalk (p. 61 (3)).

c

d

Twigs stout, rough-haired when young; buds large (2). Flowers appearing long before leaves (1). Fruits with flat rounded wings (4), often developed before the leaves: seed centrally placed. Bark smooth, silvery-grey— hence the name 'glabra'—becoming with age grey-brown and broadly furrowed. Timber strongly figured, not splitting and very resistant when wet.

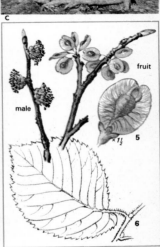

### English Elm
*Ulmus procera*

  † *

A tall tree to 30 m, which suckers freely and is often surrounded by younger trees particularly in hedgerows. Its massive branches come off high up the trunk giving a silhouette of irregular, domed, billowing branches and a narrower domed crown—a familiar feature in the English landscape, already severely threatened by the Dutch Elm disease. Botanically distinguished by its rounded dark green leaves, which are rough on the upper side, with 10–12 pairs of lateral veins and a double-toothed margin; the leaf blade (6) with the longer side rounded; the fruit (5) with the seed placed above the middle. Twigs rather stout, persistently hairy.

Many local forms of English Elm occur, and locally established 'clones' may give their own distinctive character to a region.

## ELM FAMILY

### Smoothed-Leaved Elm
*Ulmus minor (carpinifolia, campestris)*

 † *

Distinguished by its leaves which are usually broadest towards the tip—obovate to oblanceolate—and usually smooth shining green above. Leaf blade with the longer side making a right angle turn into the leaf stalk; autumn colouring yellow. Twigs usually slender, soon hairless; buds hairy (2). Fruit (1) obovate; seed placed above the middle. A suckering tree up to 30 m. There are many forms; hybridization is common, often making precise identification difficult. Some races have very distinctive narrow pyramidal crowns, such as the Cornish Elm, var. *cornubiensis*; and the Jersey Elm, var. *sarniensis*; while others like the Dutch Elm, × *hollandica*, have wide-spreading crowns. Grey-Leaved Elm, *U. canescens*, is a distinctive species of the Mediterranean region. The first year's twigs are densely and softly white-haired, and leaves grey-haired beneath.

### Fluttering Elm
*Ulmus laevis*

So called because of the unique long-stalked flowers (3) which flutter in the breeze. Leaves hairless or with soft curled hairs beneath, base very unequal; twigs hairy or hairless. Fruit (4) very long-stalked, wing ciliate. Bark flaking. A native tree to 35 m of C. and S.–E. Europe, usually in alluvial valleys.

a

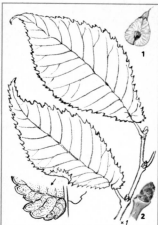

b

c

62

*Zelkova abelicea (cretica)*

A rare tree to 15 m or shrub found in the mountains of Crete. Distinguished by its tiny, almost stalkless leaves, about 2.5 cm (see p. 60), which are coarsely and irregularly toothed. Twigs slender, downy. Flowers white, sweet-scented, appearing with the leaves. Fruit unwinged, rounded, nut-like, and finely hairy.

## Nettle Tree

*Celtis australis*

  *

A rather graceful, deciduous tree to 25 m, with small ovate-lanceolate, sharp-toothed leaves often with a long twisted point. Leaf blades sharply toothed, base unequally rounded or heart-shaped, very rough above, softly hairy beneath and becoming hairless. Trunk smooth; twigs downy and flexible. Flowers long-stalked, appearing with the leaves. Fruit 9–12 mm, turning brownish-black, fleshy, sweet-tasting and edible; nut pitted (1). Native in thickets in the Mediterranean region and S. Europe; often planted for ornament and shade.

a

b

c

d

## ELM FAMILY

*Celtis tournefortii*

An uncommon shrub or small tree of woods of the Balkan peninsula and Sicily. Distinguished from the previous species by its ovate leaves which have rounded, blunt teeth. Fruit obovoid, yellowish-brown, nut 4-ridged.
*C. caucasica* reaches E. Bulgaria from Turkey. It has leaves with sharp-toothed margins and wedge-shaped bases to the leaf blades.

a

## MULBERRY FAMILY      Moraceae

Quite an important tropical and sub-tropical family of trees and shrubs, distinguished by the presence of milky juices in stems and leaves. Also by its fleshy fruits which are often encircled by fleshy lobes. Flowers one-sexed, small and inconspicuous, in dense clusters, and in the case of figs are enclosed in a fleshy urn-shaped receptacle. The family consists of about 1,000 species, approximately 600 of which are figs; none is native to Europe except perhaps the fig. A number of small ornamental trees, often with distinctive foliage and edible fruit, have been introduced to Europe.

Common Mulberry

Paper Mulberry

Fig

### Common or Black Mulberry
*Morus nigra*

  ‡

Mulberries are distinguished by their raspberry-like fruits, composed of numerous tiny fleshy berries. Common Mulberry is a small tree with stout, rough, branches, and leaves which are rough above, hairy beneath, and toothed or lobed. Fruit sweet only when ripe. A native of C. Asia; widely cultivated in S. Europe for its fruits and ornament elsewhere.

b

c

## White Mulberry
*Morus alba*

Distinguished from the preceding by hairless twigs, smooth, shining leaves, and by its long-stalked white, pinkish, or purplish fruits. They are sweet even before fully ripe. Frequently grown in S. and S.–E. Europe for its fruit and its foliage which is used to feed silk-worms. A native of China.

## Paper Mulberry
*Broussonetia papyrifera*

A small deciduous tree with large ovate, toothed, often variously lobed leaves which are grey-woolly beneath. Trees one-sexed; male flowers in pendulous catkins (c); females in dense, woolly-haired spheres (d). Fruit 2 cm across, turning orange-red. Native of E. Asia; planted for ornament in S. Europe. In Japan the bark is used for papermaking.

## Osage Orange
*Maclura pomifera*

A spiny, deciduous tree, distinguished by its large orange-like fruit 10–14 cm across, which have a milky juice and are inedible. Leaves oval-lanceolate, long-pointed. Trees one-sexed; male flowers in stalked clusters. Sometimes grown as hedges and ornament in S. Europe. Native of N. America.

a

b

c

d

e

f

## MULBERRY FAMILY

### Fig
*Ficus carica*

  † *

A small tree or shrub with smooth metallic-grey trunk and branches, and distinctive very large, deeply 3–5-lobed leaves. Leaf blades 10–20 cm, long and wide, with heart-shaped base, rough above, hairy beneath. Flowers minute (2), enclosed in a fleshy structure (1) with a small hole in the apex allowing entry to pollinating insects. Some fruits set without pollination. Green fruits appear in autumn (a) on bare branches and ripen to green, violet, or black fruits the following year—the most highly prized figs. Others form in spring (c) and ripen the same autumn. Widely grown in S. Europe for its important fruit crop. Possibly a European native, but long cultivated and often escaping into the wild in the south.

### POKEWEED FAMILY
#### Phytolaccaceae

*Phytolacca dioica*

  ‡

A small, rapidly growing, stout-branched, S. American tree; planted for ornament and shade in the Mediterranean region and locally naturalized. Leaves hairless, ovate to lanceolate, 6–12 cm. Flowers greenish, one-sexed, in drooping spikes scarcely as long as the leaves. Fruit fleshy, berry-like, purplish-black, with 7–10 carpels.

66

## BUTTERCUP FAMILY
### Ranunculaceae

**Traveller's Joy**
*Clematis vitalba*

A vigorous woody climber growing through trees and bushes to as high as 30 m. Flowers greenish-white, in terminal clusters arising from the axils of the upper leaves. They are replaced by the silvery feathery clusters of fruiting heads (b) which often remain conspicuous to the following spring, hence its popular name 'Old Man's Beard'. Leaves compound with 3–5 large, oval, stalked and often toothed leaflets. Both the leaf stalks and the individual leaflet stalks are prehensile and coil firmly round branches for support. Old climbing stems (c) may grow to the thickness of an arm with strongly grooved bark, which flakes off in strips. One of the very few true lianas native to Europe, where it is widespread; one of the only woody genera in the Buttercup family.

**Fragrant Clematis**
*Clematis flammula*

Less vigorous than the preceding climber; growing to 5 m in hedgerows and thickets in S. Europe. Distinguished by its leaves which are twice cut into numerous small oval or lanceolate leaflets. Flowers white, very fragrant. 'Petals' hairless on the upper side (hairy on both sides in the former), and the fruits are strongly compressed. *C. orientalis* has yellowish flowers. Greece, Aegean Islands.

## BUTTERCUP FAMILY

*Clematis cirrhosa* (a)
*Clematis viticella* (b)

The former is a low ever-green climber of scrub and thickets of S. Europe. Flowers yellowish-white, sometimes red-spotted, with a green calyx-like involucre. Leaves entire, lobed, or compound.
The latter is a slender decid-uous climber, with fragrant purple flowers. Leaves compound, leaflets three-lobed. Fruit with hairless styles. Native of thickets of S. Europe.

a

b

# BARBERRY FAMILY         Berberidaceae

A small family of shrubs and herbs, mostly from the N. temperate region. *Berberis* is the largest genus with about 175 species; 4 closely related species are native to Europe, only one grows to over 2 m. They are distinguished by their bright yellow wood, their 3–5 cleft spines occuring below each leaf cluster (4), their clustered, yellow flowers, and fleshy fruits. Of considerable interest are the stamens: the anthers (2) open by flap-like valves, and when an insect visits the flowers in search of nectar from the paired nectaries (1) at the base of the petals, the stamens jerk upwards depositing pollen onto its body. Fruit (3) a two-seeded berry.

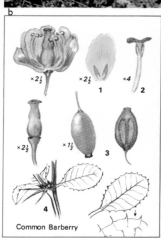

×2½   ×2½   ×4

1        2

×2½   ×1½   3

4

Common Barberry

### Common Barberry
*Berberis vulgaris*

A densely branched, spiny, deciduous shrub, growing to 3 m. From each node of the yellowish, ribbed stem (4) arise 3 stiff spines and a cluster of oval leaves with bristly-toothed margins. Flower clusters pendulous, 3–5 cm. Fruits edible. Widespread in Europe except the north; often locally exterminated because it is a host plant of Wheat Rust.

c

d

## MAGNOLIA FAMILY     Magnoliaceae

A family of trees and shrubs of Asia and America, of about 100 species, none of which is now native in Europe, though known from fossil records to have grown in Europe in the past. Leaves evergreen or deciduous, simple; stipules often enclosing bud. Flowers usually large, solitary, with numerous 'petals'; stamens and carpels arranged spirally on an elongated axis. Fruit comprising a number of fleshy or winged units which separate leaving the axis. Magnolias are widely planted for ornament in Europe, notably: *M. stellata*; *M. × soulangiana*; Evergreen Magnolia, *M. grandiflora*; Cucumber Tree, *M. acuminata*; Umbrella Tree, *M. tripetala*; Yulan, *M. denudata*.

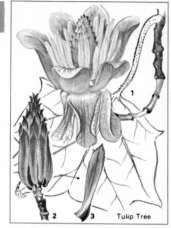

Tulip Tree

### Tulip Tree
*Liriodendron tulipifera*

A tall deciduous tree of N. America with very distinctive leaves unlike any other. Leaf blades (1) mostly four-angled cut off squarely in a broad, often notched, apex. Shoots becoming reddish; buds laterally flattened; bark grey. Flowers 6–8 cm across. Fruits (2) at length splitting into individual winged units (3). Planted for ornament and occasionally for timber in C. Europe.

a

b

## LAUREL FAMILY     Lauraceae

The laurel is the only European member of this largely tropical family of 1,000 trees and shrubs. The family is important because of the many aromatic oils that it yields, such as cinnamon, camphor, benzoin, sassafras, as well as the Avocado. They are mostly evergreen, with aromatic foliage and simple leaves. Flowers usually inconspicuous, clustered (4), often with 6 petals and up to 12 stamens; anthers with flap-like valves (5). Fruit a drupe or berry (6).

Laurel
Sweet Bay

## LAUREL FAMILY

### Laurel, Sweet Bay
*Laurus nobilis*

 †*

A dense, dark green, evergreen shrub or tree to 20 m, with very aromatic leaves when crushed (p. 69). Native of evergreen thickets and hills in the Mediterranean region, often planted elsewhere for ornament and use and sometimes naturalized. Not to be confused with Spotted or Dog Laurel (see p. 154) or Cherry Laurel (see p. 98).

## PITTOSPORUM FAMILY
### Pittosporaceae

### Karo
*Pittosporum crassifolium*

 ‡

One of several members of the small Pittosporum family, *Pittosporaceae*, which are grown for ornament in S. and W. Europe. This small tree or shrub is often planted for shelter near the coast in the west. Leaves leathery, blunt, downy beneath with inrolled margins. Fruit globular, white-woolly, with 3–4 woody valves. Native of New Zealand.

*Pittosporum tobira*

 ‡

A dense evergreen shrub often grown for ornament along the Mediterranean coast and occasionally escaping. Flowers, with very sweet orange-blossom scent, creamy then yellowish, in dense clusters 5–8 cm across; sepals hairy. Leaves obovate, leathery, dark green above, paler and hairless beneath. Native of China and Japan.

a

b

c

d

e

*Pittosporum undulatum* (a)
*Pittosporum tenuifolium* (b)

Natives of Australia and New
Zealand respectively; both are
grown in W. and S. Europe for
ornament and occasionally become naturalized. The former
has ovate-lanceolate acute,
hairless leaves; white fragrant
flowers; and orange fruits.
The latter has bright lustrous
green foliage, and black twigs,
sometimes used for winter
decoration. Flowers chocolate-
purple, honey-scented.

a

b

## PLANE FAMILY          Platanaceae

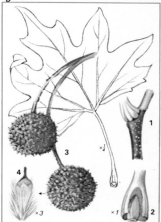

A tiny family of the northern hemisphere comprising only 8
species, with quite distinctive botanical features. The bark
flakes off in shallow plates giving the trunk the familiar mottled
appearance (c). The side buds (1) on the twigs are completely
encircled by the base of the leaf (2), and only become exposed
when the leaf falls. The numerous one-sexed flowers are clustered closely together into globular heads (p. 72) which enlarge
in fruit (3), and several of these are borne on pendulous stalks.
The hairy individual nutlets (4) are also distinctive. One species
is native in Europe.

**London Plane**
*Platanus hybrida*

A magnificent tree of rapid
growth, able to thrive under
very difficult conditions of
pollution and cramped rooting
systems in towns and industrial
areas. It can be grown in all but
the north and dryer south of
Europe, and is widely planted as
a wayside and boulevard tree,
and often pollarded into grotes-
que shapes. It is said it has
'never been known to blow
down'. The mottled greyish-

c

d

green or yellowish flaking bark, and the handsome leaves, cut to less than half-way into 5 wide-pointed lobes, must be familiar to all town dwellers. Flower clusters one-sexed; fruit with long hairs. The London Plane is not found in the wild; its origin is unknown, it is probably a hybrid, or a cultivated form of the following species. It is usually propagated by cuttings as it rarely sets good seed. The timber is fine-grained and tough and of some value.

## Oriental Plane
*Platanus orientalis*

Native tree of the Balkan peninsula in rocky valleys usually near water. Often planted in villages in S. and S.–E. Europe, where it grows to majestic proportions, providing shade and a meeting place for the inhabitants. Distinguished from the former by the much more deeply cut leaves, to beyond the middle of the blade, with narrow parallel-sided lobes which are themselves coarsely toothed. Leaves 5–7-lobed with the central lobe much longer than its width at the base. The pendulous fruits are usually in clusters of 3–6, whereas they are mostly paired in the former.

a

b

c

d

×1½ leaf base

×4

female

male ×¼

×4

leaf base ×1

fruit ×1

leaf tip

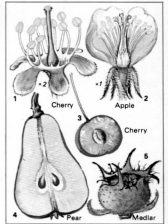

**ROSE FAMILY**             **Rosaceae**

A large and important world-wide family of about 3,200 species. In Europe there are about 60 native woody trees and shrubs over 2 m in height (excluding the roses, *Rosa*). The family shows great variety in their fruits and includes apples, pears, plums, cherries, peaches, almonds, apricots, which are of considerable economic importance, as well as others like whitebeams, hawthorns, that are of little value. Botanically the family is distinguished by its 5 sepals, sometimes with an additional set of lobes, the *epicalyx*, 5 petals, numerous stamens, and an ovary of one (1) or several (2) carpels. The ovaries and consequently the fruits may be superior (3), commonly half-inferior (5), or sometimes inferior (4).

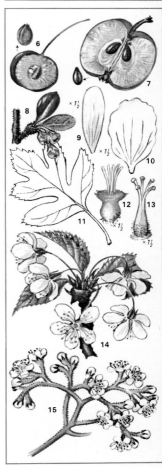

| Key to ROSE Family | ROSACEAE |
|---|---|
| 1 Carpel 1; fruit fleshy with hard stone (6). | *Prunus* (p91–8) |
| 1 Carpels 2 to many (7). | |
|   2 Fruit dry, carpels splitting. | **Nine Bark** (p74) |
|   2 Fruit fleshy, carpels not splitting. | |
|     3 Flowers solitary. | |
|       4 Flowers less than 1 cm across. | *Cotoneaster* (p85–6) |
|       4 Flowers more than 1 cm across. | **Medlar** (p86), **Quince** (p74) |
|     3 Flowers in clusters of 2 to many. | |
|       5 Walls of carpels hard, stony. | |
|         6 Leaves entire (8); stems spineless. | *Cotoneaster* (p85–6) |
|         6 Leaves toothed or lobed (11); stems spiny. | **Hawthorns** (p87–90), **Firethorn** (p86) |
|       5 Walls of carpels flexible, leathery. | |
|         7 Flowers in compound flat-topped clusters, or branched panicles (15). | *Sorbus* (p79–83), **Loquat** (p84) |
|         7 Flowers in simple umbels (14), spike-like, or in few-flowered clusters. | |
|           8 Petals narrow, not narrowed to a 'claw' (9). | **Mespilus** (p84), *Amelanchier* (p85) |
|           8 Petals rounded or ovate, narrowed to a 'claw' (10). | |
|             9 Styles free (12); fleshy fruit gritty. | **Pears** (p74–7) |
|             9 Styles fused at base (13); fruit not gritty. | **Apples** (p77–8) |

## ROSE FAMILY

### Nine Bark
*Physocarpus opulifolius*

A low, arched, deciduous shrub
to 3 m, native of N. America;
planted for ornament and sometimes naturalized. Leaves rounded to ovate, toothed, often
shallow lobed. Bark smooth,
peeling. Flowers white tinged
with pink, in hemispherical
clusters, 2.5–5 cm across. Fruit
usually of 4–5 splitting, inflated carpels (1).

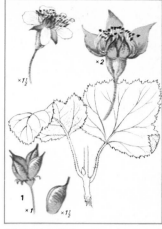

### Quince
*Cydonia oblonga*

An Asian shrub or small tree
widely cultivated in Europe and
often naturalized in the south.
Leaves becoming dark green
above, white-woolly beneath.
Fruit 2.5–3.5 cm in the wild,
larger under cultivation and
used for making preserves.
The Japonica *Chaenomeles
speciosa,* and *C. japonica*, with
red flowers, are often planted
and sometimes found as escapes.

a

### Key to PEARS (*Pyrus*)

1 Fruit with deciduous calyx (2).   *cordata* (p75)
1 Fruit with persistent calyx.
  2 Fruit large, 6–16 cm, fleshy.   **Common** (p75)
  2 Fruit up to 5.5 cm, hard.
   3 Leaves not more than 1½   **Wild** (p75)
    times longer than broad (3).
   3 Leaves more than 1½ times
    longer than broad (5).
    4 Mature leaves hairless, with   **Almond-Leaved** (p76)
     fine swellings beneath.
    4 Mature leaves hairy or
     woolly beneath (5).
     5 Styles densely shaggy-   *nivalis* (p77), *elaeagrifolia*
      haired, at least at base (4).   (p76)
     5 Styles more or less hairless.   *salvifolia* (p76)

b

c

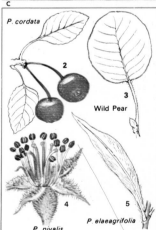

## Common Pear
*Pyrus communis*

  † *

A tree to 20 m with straight trunk, spreading branches (which may or may not be spiny), suckering freely and often forming thickets round the parent tree. Flowers, in domed clusters with conspicuous red to purple anthers, opening before or at the same time as the leaves; flower stalks woolly. Leaves ovate to elliptic with a toothed or entire margin; usually hairless when mature. Fruit variable, pear-shaped, top-shaped, globular, or oblong, sweet when ripe. Probably a tree of hybrid origin: there are around 1,000 different cultivated varieties. Grown for its fruits for at least 2,000 years. *P. cordata* is a spiny shrub or small tree of thickets and hedges of W. Europe with smaller flowers with petals 6–8 mm. Fruit tiny 8–15 mm, shining red, densely covered with lenticels (p. 74 (2)); calyx at length falling.

## Wild Pear
*Pyrus pyraster*

Distinguished from Common Pear by its small, hard, rounded fruit 1.3–3.5 cm, turning yellow, brown, or black when ripe. Leaves variable, elliptic to rounded, with a wedge-shaped, rounded, or heart-shaped base, toothed or entire (p. 74 (3)). A small, usually spiny, tree of C., S., and W. Europe. One of several parents of the cultivated pear.

a

b

c

d

e

seed

## Almond-Leaved Pear
### *Pyrus amygdaliformis*

Distinguished by its narrow, usually toothless leaves which become hairless and minutely pimpled beneath. Twigs grey-woolly when young. Fruit 1.5–3 cm; fruit stalk stout, about as long as or longer than fruit. A shrub or small tree to 6 m, sometimes spiny, found in dry rocky places in the Mediterranean region.

*P. salvifolia* has similar leaves but becoming almost hairless above and grey-woolly beneath. Styles almost hairless. It is found in dry, open woods, or sunny slopes from Belgium eastwards to Greece and often cultivated in this region for its fruit.

a

b

### *Pyrus elaeagrifolia*

A shrub or small tree, with stout spiny branches, of dry places in S.–E. Europe. Twigs grey-woolly, and leaves densely greyish- to white-haired. Flower clusters with white-woolly hairs, nearly stalkless. Petals about 1 cm; styles densely woolly below. Fruit rounded or pear-shaped, 2–3 cm across when ripe.

c

young fruits

*Pyrus nivalis*

An attractive tree to 20 m with white-woolly young shoots, leaves, and flower clusters, particularly distinctive in spring. Leaves later becoming sparsely hairy above, greyish beneath. Petals white, 14–16 mm; styles shaggy-haired only at base (p. 74 (4)). Ripe fruit yellowish-green with purple dots, becoming sweet. Found in dry places, open woods in S. and S.–C. Europe.

## Crab Apple
*Malus sylvestris*

One of several parental species of the orchard Apple, from which it can usually be distinguished by the hairless or almost hairless mature leaves, and small, very sour fruit. A spiny, intricately branched shrub or small tree to 10 m, found throughout Europe in hedges and thickets. Also often grown as a rootstock for grafting. Leaves ovate to elliptic with a rounded or wedge-shaped base, short-pointed apex, and toothed margin. Flowers white or pink. Fruit 2.5–3 cm, green to yellow. Wood fine-grained, brownish, and very hard and strong.

# ROSE FAMILY

## Apple
### *Malus domestica*

Over 1,000 cultivated varieties
are known, involving both
European and Asiatic species.
Grown in orchards and gardens
for its fruit, often escaping to
hedgerows and thickets. Distinguished by its leaves, which
are slightly woolly above,
densely so below, and its large,
variously green to red, sweet or
sour fruit.

### *Malus trilobata*

A shrub or small erect-branched
tree native of Turkey, which
penetrates as far west as N.–E.
Greece. Its distinctive deeply
three-lobed, lustrous leaves re-
call the Field Maple, but its
clustered white flowers each
3.5 cm across and its yellowish-
green fleshy ripe fruit are un-
mistakably apple-like. Twigs at
first downy, then hairless;
autumn colouring good.

### *Malus florentina*

A small, rounded, spineless, very
local tree of Italy, Yugoslavia,
and N. Greece. Leaves and fruits
recalling some hawthorns. Leaves
broadly ovate with irregular
shallow lobes, white-woolly
beneath; leaf stalk short 0.5–2
cm. Flowers white, 1.5–2 cm
across. Fruit small, about 1 cm,
red when ripe, without calyx.

Beauty of Bath

a

b

c

M. trilobata

×1

×1

M. florentina

d

# WHITEBEAMS, SERVICE TREES ROWANS

# SORBUS

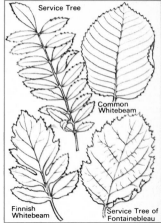

Service Tree

Common Whitebeam

Finnish Whitebeam

Service Tree of Fontainebleau

Probably the most difficult genus of woody trees in Europe to identify; over 90 species have been described. Owing to hybridization and restricted breeding systems, hybrid complexes of many closely related forms have evolved in different geographical regions. The most important diagnostic characters are those of leaf lobing and toothing; fruit colour and distribution of the lenticels on fruit. The pinnate-leaved species include Service Tree and Rowan; entire-leaved species include some whitebeams (*S. aria* and *S. graeca*), and species with distinctly lobed leaves include Finnish Whitebeam and Wild Service Tree.

## Service Tree
*Sorbus domestica*

   †

A handsome slow-growing tree to 15 m, with distinctive pinnate leaves, each with 13–17 neat toothed leaflets. Branches more spreading, and bark shredding, in contrast to the Rowan with which it might well be confused when not fruiting. Winter buds hairless, sticky, and shining. Flowers 1.5–2 cm across, in domed clusters; sepals triangular; styles 5. Fruits like small pears or globular, varying from greenish to brownish, hard and very astringent to the taste. Only edible when frosted, or over-ripe and used for making alcoholic beverages. Wood tough, resistant to friction. A native tree of most of S. Europe; often planted for its fruit and for ornament in C. Europe and locally naturalized.

×1

×2

a

b

c

# ROSE FAMILY

## Rowan, Mountain Ash
*Sorbus aucuparia*

  *

A beautiful small tree to 15 m
with smooth, shining, grey bark,
up-spreading branches, and pinnate leaves. It is widely distributed throughout Europe in
open woods, thickets, heaths,
and on rocky slopes and in mountain woods where it thrives up
to the tree line at about 2,000 m
in C. Europe. Leaves with 11–
15 toothed leaflets, becoming
hairless; buds (1) stout, grey-
haired, not sticky. Flowers
strong-smelling, in usually wool-
ly-stemmed clusters 10–15 cm
across; styles 3–4. Fruits at first
yellow then suddenly turning
orange to scarlet—the first sorbus to colour in autumn. Fruit
edible but sour and pungent;
the wood is dense and hard.
Many superstitions surround
this tree in N. Europe.

## Wild Service Tree
*Sorbus torminalis*

Unlike other sorbuses in having
palmately-lobed, plane-like
leaves which at length become
hairless beneath. Leaf blades
with 3–4 pairs of triangular
toothed lobes which become
progressively smaller towards
the apex. Twigs shining brown;
buds shining green, globular (2).
Flower clusters rather open,
domed, about 10–12 cm across;
flowers white; styles 2. Fruit
leathery brown and dotted with

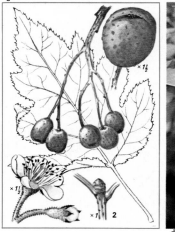

lenticels, in long-stalked clusters. A medium sized tree to 25 m, with ascending branches and scaly bark; widely scattered throughout Europe except in the north. Well known for its fruits which were used medicinally in the past.

## Common Whitebeam
*Sorbus aria*

  † *

A distinctive tree to 25 m with domed crown, up-swept branches, and smooth grey trunk. In spring only the white woolly undersides of the leaves are visible, and from a distance the whole tree looks white as though it were in blossom (d)—hence its name. Widely distributed in woods and rocky places, and in mountains in the south; related species occur in Scandinavia. The ovate to elliptic leaves (p. 79) are irregularly double-toothed (1), the acute teeth curved forwards towards the tip of the blade; sometimes the margin is shallowly lobed. Buds large, green, sometimes hairy (2). Flower clusters 5–8 cm across, with white woolly stalks. Fruit 8–15 mm, usually longer than wide with usually numerous small lenticels.

## ROSE FAMILY

### Sorbus umbellata

This sorbus, native of the Balkan peninsula, has yellowish fruits about 1.5 cm across. Leaves shallowly lobed, densely white-woolly beneath, with only 4–7 pairs of lateral veins.

### Finnish Whitebeam
#### Sorbus hybrida

Distinguished by its leaves (p. 79) which are deeply lobed, with 2 pairs of quite free leaflets at the base and lobes becoming progressively shallower towards the apex (p. 79). Fruit globular 10–12 mm, red, with small scattered lenticels. A medium sized tree of Scandinavia and Finland.

### Sorbus mougeotii

A shrub or tree of the western Alps and Pyrenees with shallowly lobed leaves cut to about $\frac{1}{4}$ of the distance to the mid-vein, the lobes not over-lapping. Leaf blades green and hairless above, grey-woolly beneath. Fruit globular, red, with small sparse lenticels. Found on high mountain slopes.

S. mougeotii

S. austriaca

S. umbellata

Greek Whitebeam

a

b

c

d

*Sorbus austriaca*

This has broader ovate leaves than the previous species, with lobes cut to about ⅓ of the way to the mid-vein, and usually somewhat overlapping each other at the margins. Fruit with rather large, numerous lenticels. Greek Whitebeam (p. 82) of S.–E. and S.–C. Europe has unlobed leaves broadest above the middle and with wedge-shaped bases. Fruit globular, scarlet, with a few large lenticels.

## Swedish Whitebeam
*Sorbus intermedia*

  *

A small to medium-sized tree with a dense rounded crown and dark glossy leaves which are lobed in the lower half, coarsely toothed above, and have yellowish-grey felted undersides. Fruit scarlet, with a few small lenticels. Native of Scandinavia and the Baltic region; widely planted as an ornamental tree; can withstand polluted atmospheres.

## Service Tree of Fontainebleau
*Sorbus latifolia*

Distinguished by its fruits which are yellowish-brown with numerous large lenticels, indicating a close relationship with the Wild Service Tree. Leaves broadly elliptical (p. 79) with 14–20 shallow triangular lobes, rounded at base, becoming hairless above, greenish-grey felted beneath. Native of W.–C. Europe. There are many related microspecies differing in fruit colour and leaf hairiness.

# ROSE FAMILY

## Loquat
*Eriobotrya japonica*

A distinctive small evergreen tree to 10 m, with large, dark green, laurel-like leaves. Often planted for its fruit and sometimes for ornament in S. Europe. Leaves firm, leathery, conspicuously veined, 12–25 cm, with reddish-brown or greyish felted hairs beneath. Twigs remaining hairy. Flowers white, fragrant, about 1 cm across, partially hidden by dense brown woolly hairs, in tight-branched, brown-stemmed pyramidal clusters. Fruit golden-yellow, elliptic or pear-shaped, 3–6 cm long, sweet and edible. Nut large, brown, smooth. A native of China; sometimes cultivated in orchards. The fruit is sold in the town and village markets of the Mediterranean region.

a

b

c

## Snowy Mespilus
*Amelanchier ovalis*

So called because of its snowy white flowers and white-felted twigs and leaves on first opening in spring. A small shrub to 4 m, with slender usually erect branches and blackish bark. Leaves ovate to obovate, rounded, notched, or pointed at the tip, coarsely toothed, at first white-felted beneath but soon hairless. Flowers distinguished by their narrow, widely-spaced petals (1), unlike other members

d

of the rose family; styles 5.
Fruit small, sweet, and edible.
Native of open woods, rocks and
stony slopes mainly on lime-
stone mountains of S. and C.
Europe.

a

## *Amelanchier grandiflora*

Distinguished by its young leaves
which are purplish, usually
nodding flower clusters, and
longish petals 1.5–1.8 cm.
The closely related *A. spicata*
has densely white-woolly young
leaves, erect flower clusters, and
shorter petals, 4–10 mm. Both
are N. American species and are
grown for ornament and sometimes naturalized.

## *Cotoneaster nebrodensis*
*(tomentosus)*

Several similar-looking related
small shrubs are native in
Europe but they rarely reach
2 m. This shrub, which grows in
dry stony places mainly in the
mountains of S. and S.–E.
Europe, may grow to 3 m. Leaves
greyish or white-felted beneath.
Flowers pinkish, in nodding
clusters of 3–12. Fruit with
whitish hairs; nuts 3–5.

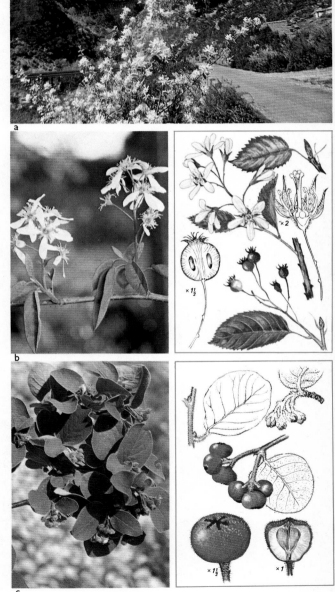

b

c

85

# ROSE FAMILY

## *Cotoneaster simonsii*

  ‡

A small deciduous or semi-evergreen shrub to 4 m, from Assam,
India; often grown for ornament
and sometimes naturalized in
N.–W. Europe. Flowers in short
clusters of 2–4. Fruit scarlet,
with 3–4 nuts. Upper side of
leaves dark green, hairy when
young; underside paler, with
sparse, stiff hairs (1).
Other species are sometimes
locally naturalized.

## Firethorn
### *Pyracantha coccinea*

A very dense, spiny, evergreen
shrub to 2 m or more, with finely toothed, hairless or sparsely
hairy leaves. Flowers white, in
dense, flat-topped clusters 2.5–4
cm across. Fruit usually bright
red, rarely orange. Native in
hedges and thickets in S. Europe;
related species and hybrids
often grown for ornament
elsewhere.

## Medlar
### *Mespilus germanica*

A deciduous shrub or small
spreading tree to 6 m, with distinctive leathery-looking, nearly
stalkless, oblong-lanceolate
leaves. A native of S.–E. Europe
which has long been cultivated
in W. and C. Europe for its
fruits, and which is often naturalized in woods and hedges.
Leaves often finely toothed,
hairy or sometimes hairless
above, downy and paler beneath.
Young twigs very hairy, older

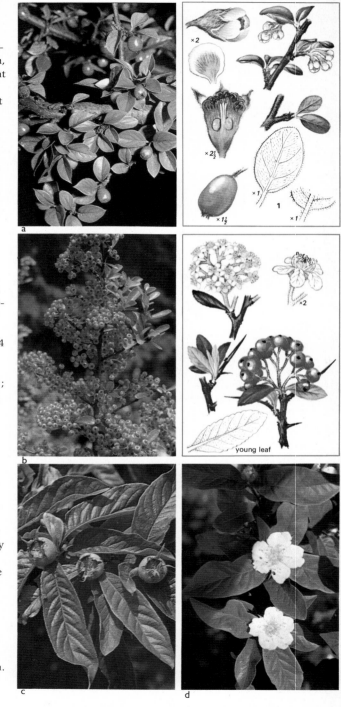

ᴸwigs often with spines; bark flaking with vertical plates. Flowers large, 3–4 cm, stalkless, nestling amongst leaves. Fruit globular, with a sunken apex surrounded by the long persisting sepals. The wood is hard and fine grained. The fruits are edible only when over-ripe or frosted; they make a good conserve.

a

**Key to HAWTHORNS** (*Crataegus*)

1 Young twigs, leaves, flower-stalks hairless (3), or with straight spreading hairs.

  2 Leaf-lobes saw-toothed; stipules saw-toothed (4).

    3 Style 1; fruit with 1 nut.          *calycina* (p88)

    3 Styles 2–3; fruit with 2 nuts (6).         **Midland Thorn** (p88)

  2 Leaf-lobes entire, or with a few teeth; stipules entire; styles 1 (7).     **Common Hawthorn** (p88)

1 Young twigs, leaves, and flower stalks with curled or adpressed woolly or silky hairs (2).

  4 Leaf stalk 1–3 cm; leaf lobes saw-toothed; flowers 1–1.5 cm across; ripe fruit blackish.     *pentagyna* (p89), *nigra* (p89)

  4 Leaf stalk 0.2–1 cm; leaf lobes entire or with 1–3 teeth at apex (1) (5); flowers 1.5–2 cm across; fruit not blackish.

    5 Leaves not more than 3 cm; fruit 7–10 mm across.     *heldreichii* (p90)

    5 Leaves 3–5 cm; fruit 1.5–2 cm across.

      6 Fruit dark red-purple.     *schraderana* (p90)

      6 Fruit orange-red to yellow.     *laciniata* (p89), **Azarole** (p89)

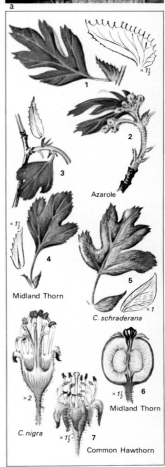

1

×1½

2

3

Azarole

×1½

4

5

Midland Thorn

*C. schraderana*

×1

×2

×1½

6

Midland Thorn

*C. nigra*    ×1½    7

Common Hawthorn

The identification of species is difficult; hybridization is common. In the key above, leaf and stipule shape, and size are from the flowering shoots; American species which are often cultivated and occasionally naturalized are excluded. Also local species: *C. macrocarpa,* E. Alps; *C. pycnoloba,* S. Greece.

## ROSE FAMILY

### Common Hawthorn
*Crataegus monogyna*

  *

The most ubiquitous of all European hawthorns. A very variable, very spiny shrub or small tree to 10 m. It is common in thickets and on the edge of woods, and colonizes grassy slopes. Widely planted as a field or roadside hedge where it can be clipped annually or allowed to grow into small trees. Leaves very variable, with 3–7 shallow or deep, blunt or acute lobes which are entire or with a few teeth towards the apex. Twigs reddish-brown, later grey, hairless or sparsely hairy; spines 1–2 cm. Flowers 8–15 mm across; style 1. Flower clusters with a pungent smell. Fruit with only one nut (crush between fingers) and variably coloured from bright red to purplish-red. Bark flaking; wood heavy and dense.

### Midland Thorn
*Crataegus laevigata (oxyacantha)*

Differing from the previous species in leaves, styles, and nuts. Leaves with 3–5 short, broad, blunt lobes with finely toothed margins. Styles 2–3. Fruit deep red; nuts 2 (p. 87). *C. calycina* has broad, acute leaf lobes, also with finely toothed margins. Flowers larger than the preceding, 1.5–2 cm across. Fruit usually cylindrical; nut 1. Both occur in N. and C. Europe.

*Crataegus pentagyna*

Distinguished by its dull black to blackish-purple fruit when ripe, with 4–5 nuts. Also by its 3–7-lobed leaves with cobwebby hairs beneath and its many-flowered clusters.
*C. nigra* has 7–11-lobed leaves, woolly-haired on both surfaces; few-flowered clusters; and lustrous black fruits with 4–5 nuts. Both are native in the woods of E.–C. Europe.

a

**Azarole**
*Crataegus azarolus*

Distinguished by its large globular orange-red or yellow fruits 2–2.5 cm, with 1–3 nuts. Leaves usually with 3 blunt often untoothed lobes, with curled adpressed hairs. Inflorescence densely felted (p. 87); styles 1–2. A shrub or small tree of hillsides and mountains of Crete; often cultivated for its edible fruit in S. Europe.

b

c

*Crataegus laciniata (orientalis)*

A shrub or small tree of thickets and rocky slopes of mountains of S.–E. Europe and Spain, with deeply cut, greyish-green, downy leaves and relatively large coral-red or orange-red fruit. Leaves with 3–7 narrow, acute, toothed lobes. Young twigs woolly, becoming blackish; spines few. Flowers 1.5–2 cm; styles 3–5. Fruit pear-shaped or globular, 1.5–2 cm.

d

# ROSE FAMILY

*Crataegus schraderana* (a)
*Crataegus heldreichii* (b)

The former is a rare shrub from the mountains of Greece with characteristically dark red-purple fruit with 2–4 nuts. Leaves and twigs (p. 87) grey-hairy at first, soon hairless. Flowers white, 15–18 mm across.
The latter is found in Greece, Albania, and Crete. It has small, globular, red fruits about 7 mm, with 1–3 nuts. Leaves and twigs covered with woolly hairs.

*Crataegus mollis* (c)
*Crataegus submollis* (d)

  ‡

Several N. American thorns with red fruits and entire or lobed leaves are grown for ornament and occasionally naturalized. The former has young leaves densely hairy beneath.
The latter has large, bright orange-red fruits.
*C. intricata* has lobed leaves and reddish-brown fruit. All three are often incorrectly named 'coccinea'.

## Cockspur Thorn
*Crataegus crus-galli*

  ‡

A small, ornamental N. American tree or shrub with dark green obovate, sharply toothed, rather leathery leaves and very long, slender spines, 7–10 cm. Leaves and twigs hairless. Flowers in erect clusters on hairless branches. Grown for ornament (particularly autumn colouring); sometimes naturalized in C. Europe.

a

b

c

d

e

90

**Key to CHERRIES, PLUMS, PEACHES, etc.** (*Prunus*)

1 Fruit and ovary hairy (1).

  2 Leaves broadly ovate, or     **Apricot** (p92)
rounded (3).

  2 Leaves at least twice as long as   **Almond** (p91), **Peach**
wide (7).   (92), *webbii* (p92)

1 Fruit and ovary hairless (6).

  3 Flowers solitary (4) (5), or in
clusters, or umbels (9).

    4 Fruit stalk at least twice as   **Cherry** (p95),
long as ripe fruit (8).   **Sour Cherry** (p95)

    4 Fruit stalk shorter than ripe
fruit, or only slightly longer
(6).

     5 Leaves hairless.   **Sloe** (p93), *cocomilia* (p94)

     5 Leaves hairy, at least on the
veins beneath.

      6 Young twigs dull, usually   **Sloe** (p93), **Plum** (p94)
hairy (5).

      6 Young twigs glossy, hairless  *brigantina* (p94), **Cherry**
(2).   **Plum** (p93)

  3 Flowers in elongated spike-like
(10), or domed clusters (11).

    7 Flowers 3–10, in short or   **St. Lucie Cherry** (p96)
domed clusters (11).

    7 Flowers 12–100, in elongated
clusters (10).

     8 Leaves evergreen, leathery;  **Portugal Laurel** (p98),
fruit with a pointed apex.  **Cherry Laurel** (p98)

     8 Leaves deciduous, thin; fruit  **Bird Cherry** (p96),
with rounded apex.   **Black Cherry** (p97),
  **Virginian Bird Cherry**
  (p97)

*P. ramburii* is local in S. Spain.

## Almond
*Prunus dulcis (Amygdalus communis)*

  ‡ *

A native tree of Asia and N. Africa long under cultivation in southern orchards and gardens for its edible nuts, and grown for ornament further north. Wild trees, unlike cultivated specimens, have spiny branches. Leaves toothed, folded in a V. Flowers appear before the leaves, harbingers of spring in the Mediterranean. Nuts (1) enclosed in tough green 'pericarp'.

a

b

# ROSE FAMILY

## Apricot
### *Prunus armeniaca*

  ‡

Well known for its reddish-orange to yellow, velvety fruit. Distinguished from peach by its broader, longer-stalked leaves. Also by the smooth stone easily separated from the flesh of the fruit. Young twigs and young leaves reddish. Flowers white or very pale pink. Native of Asia; grown as a field crop for its fruits in S. Europe.

## Peach
### *Prunus persica* (c)

  ‡

### *Prunus webbii* (d)

When in fruit there is no mistaking the familiar small tree which came originally from China, and is now grown widely in orchards in S. and S.–C. Europe, and in gardens further north. Occasionally naturalized in the south. Its delicious edible fruit has an exquisite aroma, yellow or pale green flesh, velvety skin and very deeply furrowed nut adhering to the flesh. Leaves lanceolate, without basal glands, finely toothed, almost hairless; twigs reddish-green, angular, hairless and without spines. Flowers pink, occasionally white, appearing with the young leaves, later than the Almond.

*P. webbii* is like a spiny wild almond with narrow leaves only 6–9 mm wide, and fruit green 2–2.5 cm. Flowers deep pink. Found in rocky places in the Balkan peninsula.

a

b

c

d

92

## Blackthorn, Sloe
*Prunus spinosa*

  † *

The most widely distributed
European prunus, failing to
reach only Iceland and the far
north. It is found on dry banks,
hillsides, and in scrub, forest
verges, and hedges. A dense,
intricately branched, very spiny
shrub to 4 m with dark blackish-
brown branches. It suckers
freely often forming thickets.
Young twigs usually hairy.
Leaves small 2–4 cm, finely
toothed, dull green, hairless
above. Flowers usually appearing long before the leaves,
but sometimes with the young
leaves. Flowers 1–1.5 cm, mostly
solitary, on short hairless stalks
about 5 mm but densely clustered on shoots. The small,
bloomed, bluish-black fruits,
1.5–2 cm, are unmistakable and
very astringent.

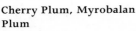

## Cherry Plum, Myrobalan Plum
*Prunus cerasifera*

Usually the first white-flowered
species to flower in the spring.
Similar to Sloe but a small
spreading tree of hedges and
thickets with glossy green,
smooth twigs (p. 94 (1)) which
are occasionally spiny. Leaves
4–7 cm, glossy above. Flowers
larger than Sloe, 2 cm across,
mostly solitary; flower stalks
about 1.5 cm. Fruit edible, 2–3
cm, at first green then yellow or

## ROSE FAMILY

red; nut globular, smooth and keeled. A native of the Balkan peninsula. Sometimes planted in C. Europe for its fruit, as a hedge shrub, and as a rootstock for grafting. Early flowering cultivated varieties with white or pink flowers and purplish-red leaves are often grown for ornament.

*Prunus brigantina* (b)

*Prunus cocomilia* (c)

The former, a shrub or small tree of dry slopes in the S.–W. Alps, has glossy hairless twigs, and strongly, irregularly cut leaves, which are downy on the veins beneath. Fruit about 2.5 cm, yellow, sour.
The latter is quite hairless. Flowers white, in clusters of 2–4, appearing with the leaves.

**Plum, Damson, Greengage**
*Prunus domestica*

  *

Probably a hybrid between Sloe and Cherry Plum. There are numerous cultivated forms widely grown and naturalized in Europe. Plums (d) have nearly hairless young twigs, greenish-white flowers, and ellipsoid fruit, 4–7.5 cm, varying from black-purple to red. Damsons have purple, Greengages, yellow to green fruits. Both have hairy young twigs and white flowers.

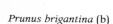

94

## Wild Cherry, Gean
*Prunus avium*

  † *

A handsome slender tree to
20 m, with up-spreading
branches and shining, reddish-
brown bark which peels off
horizontally in strips. Native
throughout Europe, except the
extreme north and Mediterranean region, growing in woods,
thickets, and hedges. Widely
grown in many cultivated forms
for its sweet fruit, ranging in
colour from black and red to
white. Leaves dull above,
drooping when young, with
two conspicuous glands (2).
Flowers in umbels with scales
at base mostly papery (1);
petals obovate. In wild trees
fruit sweet or bitter, bright or
dark red; nut smooth. Wood
tough, straight-grained,
reddish-brown.

## Sour Cherry
*Prunus cerasus*

  ‡

Like Wild Cherry but usually a
bush, and with dark green,
glossy, spreading leaves (young
leaves drooping in Wild Cherry),
and usually bright red, acid
fruit. Scales at the base of the
inflorescence mostly leaf-like;
petals rounded; receptacle
cup-shaped. Native of Asia;
grown for its fruit, the Morello
Cherry, and widely naturalized.

# ROSE FAMILY

## St. Lucie Cherry
### *Prunus mahaleb*

A much branched spreading
shrub, rarely a tree, of dry
hills, thickets and open woods
of C. and S. Europe, with small
white flowers and small black
fruits. It can be recognized by
the small, domed, branched
axillary clusters, 3–4 cm long,
of 3–10 flowers, borne on short
leafy side-shoots (1). Leaves
broadly ovate, toothed, glossy,
hairless or finely hairy beneath.
Young twigs greyish, glandular,
becoming brownish, with pale
lenticels. Flowers sweet-scented,
1–1.5 cm. Fruit bitter, 8–10 mm.
Wood aromatic, due to coumarin
which gives the scent to new-
mown hay; hence the flavour
of cherrywood pipes made from
this species.

a

b

## Bird Cherry
### *Prunus padus*

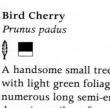

A handsome small tree to 15 m,
with light green foliage and
numerous long semi–erect or
drooping spikes of small fragrant
white flowers arising from the
side shoots. A native woodland
tree of most of Europe except
the Mediterranean and Balkans.
It also occurs as a low shrub to
3m in the north and in mountains of C. Europe. Leaves
6–10 cm, finely toothed, dull
green above; young branches

c

d

finely hairy or hairless; buds slender, pointed. Flower clusters with a few leaves at the base (1). Fruit shining black, rich in tannin and consequently very astringent. Bark and wood with a strong disagreeable odour; bark smooth, dark grey-brown.

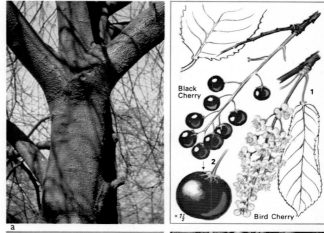

## Black Cherry
*Prunus serotina*

 ‡*

Like Bird Cherry in general appearance, but distinguished by its glossy, dark green leaves with incurved marginal teeth; its larger flowers, about 1 cm across; and its purplish-black fruits which have a persistent calyx (2). A native tree of N. America, planted for timber in C. Europe and for ornament elsewhere and sometimes becoming naturalized. The bark is very aromatic.

Virginian Bird Cherry, *P. virginiana*, is occasionally planted in C. Europe and naturalized. It has dark red fruit, and a calyx which does not persist but falls off. A shrub to 5 m with bark which is not aromatic. Leaves dull, with very acute, more spreading marginal teeth and 8–11 conspicuous lateral veins (at least 15 in Black Cherry).

## ROSE FAMILY

### Portugal Laurel
*Prunus lusitanica*

A dense, sombre, evergreen bush or tree to 8 m or more, with large glossy leaves, and long spikes of flowers, longer than the subtending leaves. A native of the Iberian peninsula, often planted for ornament in the west. Bark black, smooth; twigs, leaf stalks, and buds red-purple above, hairless. Flowers very fragrant, 1–1.5 cm. Fruit 8–13 mm, turning purplish-black.

### Cherry Laurel
*Prunus laurocerasus*

Often mistakenly called laurel because of its large shiny ever-green leaves up to 20 cm. A native of S.–E. Europe, but frequently grown for ornament and cover in the S. and W., and sometimes naturalized. Bark brown-grey. Twigs, leaf stalks, and buds green. Flower clusters erect, about as long as subtending leaves. Leaves contain prussic acid.

a

b

c

d

## PEA FAMILY                Leguminosae

One of the three largest families, with as many as 13,000 species. It is cosmopolitan and supplies valuable products such as food, fodder, gums, resins, timber, and its nitrogen-fixing ability is important in maintaining soil fertility. Botanically distinguished by its compound (4), alternate leaves, its pod-like fruits (5) (6) splitting into 2 valves, and its flowers. These are either small, regular, with numerous stamens (2), or irregular (3) with un-equal petals and 10 stamens (1). Most European species have pea-shaped irregular flowers (3) with petals comprising a standard, 2 wings, and a keel (see p. 110 (3)), and 10 stamens fused by their filaments (1). Most European species are her-baceous, few are large woody plants; many are ornamental.

## Key to PEA Family

1 Stamens numerous, projecting (2); petals small or absent.

1 Stamens enclosed in pea-like flowers (4); standard, wings and keel conspicuous.

  2 Stamens 5–10, not fused by their filaments (3).

  2 Stamens 10, fused by their filaments into a tube (1).

    3 Flowers yellow.

      4 Spiny shrubs over 2 metres.

      4 Spineless trees, or shrubs over 2 metres.

        5 Slender switch-like shrubs, often without leaves.

        5 Shrubs or trees, leafy throughout.

          6 Leaves trifoliate (9); or with 1 leaflet (6).

          6 Leaves pinnate (7) with 2 or more pairs of leaflets or digitate (5).

    3 Flowers white, purple, violet or pink.

**LEGUMINOSAE**

Carob (p100), **Honey-Locust** (p101), *Acacia* (p101–4), **Persian Acacia** (p105)

**Judas Tree** (p99), **Pagoda Tree** (p105), **Bean Trefoil** (p106)

**Gorse** (p110), **Spiny Brooms** (p107)

**Spanish Broom** (p110), **Brooms** (p108–9) *Lygos* (p109)

**Medick** (p113), *Adeno-carpus* (p111) *Petteria* (p110), **Brooms** (p108–9), **Laburnums** (p106–7) **Bladder Senna** (p112), **Lupin** (p111)

**False Acacia** (p111), **Wisteria** (p112), **False Indigo** (p113), *Lygos* (p109), **White Spanish Broom** (p108)

## Judas Tree
*Cercis siliquastrum*

A small deciduous tree to 10 m, quite unlike any other member of the family, with entire rounded leaves, beautiful pink flowers, and reddish-brown pods. A native of the E. Mediterranean extending as far west as France, often planted and grown for ornament elsewhere in the south. In the wild it grows on rocky slopes, in dry woods and by streams. Leaves, 7–12 cm, rounded or notched at

a

apex, with a heart-shaped base
(1). Flowers usually appearing
before the leaves, in clusters on
old branches; petals irregular,
the upper petals smaller (2);
stamens 10, not fused by their
filaments. Pod red-purple when
young. Bark brown, finely
fissured.

### Carob, Locust Tree
*Ceratonia siliqua*

 *

A dense, dark evergreen, domed
tree to 10 m, casting a heavy
shade, or often seen as clumped
bushes. A native tree of the
drier regions of the Mediterranean where it stands out in
contrast with the paler grey-
green foliage of the olives in an
otherwise parched brown summer landscape. It is widely cultivated, often on terraces, for its
pods which are used for both
cattle fodder and human con-
sumption. When ripe the pods
turn chocolate brown and are
sweet to the taste; the seeds are
the original 'carat' weight.
Leaves compound with 2–5
pairs of large leathery, rounded,
glossy leaflets. Flowers appearing in the autumn (c). Pods up
to 20 cm long, found at most
times of the year on older branches. Wood hard, reddish and
lustrous.

**Honey-Locust**
*Gleditsia triacanthos*

  ‡

A native deciduous tree of N.
America, often planted for
ornament in C. and S. Europe.
Unique in usually having
fearsome clusters of branched
spines arising from the trunk.
Leaves pinnate or twice-pinnate
with numerous toothed leaflets.
Flowers fragrant, in axillary
clusters. Pods long, 30–45 cm by
2–3 cm, sickle shaped or spirally
twisted.

a

b

**Key to ACACIAS, WATTLES (*Acacia*)**

1  Leaves all twice pinnate.

  2  Leaves deciduous; twigs spiny. **Opoponax** (p102), *karoo* (p102)

  2  Leaves evergreen; twigs not spiny. **Silver Wattle** (p102), *mearnsii* (p102)

1  At least some leaves simple, long and narrow.

  3  Flowers in long axillary spikes; fruits rounded in section. **Sydney Golden Wattle** (p103)

  3  Flowers in stalked, rounded clusters; fruit flattened in section.

    4  Leaves with 2–6 longitudinal veins; fruit twisted. **Blackwood Acacia** (p103), *cyclops* (p104)

    4  Leaves with 1 longitudinal vein; fruit nearly straight.

     5  Leaves conspicuously sickle-shaped; flower heads 10–20 in each cluster. **Golden Wattle** (p104)

     5  Leaves more or less straight; flower heads 2–10 in each cluster. **Blue-Leaved Wattle** (p103), *retinodes* (p104)

The majority are natives of Australia and Tasmania and are
grown for ornament, soil stabilization, and occasionally for
timber in S. Europe particularly along the Mediterranean coast-
line. They sometimes become naturalized.

Silver Wattle

*A. retinodes*

Sydney Golden Wattle

*A. karoo*

Blue-Leaved Wattle

*A. cyclops*

# PEA FAMILY

*Acacia karoo*

  ‡

Unmistakable with its extremely
long stout spines which are
5–10 cm. Leaves twice-pinnate,
with leaflets 6–10 mm (p. 101).
Flower heads yellow, in clusters
of 4–6, in the axils of the upper
leaves, slightly fragrant. Pod
8–13 cm, flattened and
constricted between seeds.
Native of S. Africa; grown for
hedges and ornament in S.–W.
Europe, and sometimes
naturalized.

## Opoponax
*Acacia farnesiana*

   ‡

A spiny shrub to 4 m with
twice-pinnate leaves and short-
stalked clusters of fragrant
flowers. Leaflets tiny 3–5 mm,
linear-oblong. Spines on old
branches 2.5 cm. Flower heads
10–12 mm, in clusters of 2–3.
Pod cylindrical, inflated, 5–9
cm. A native of Dominica, West
Indies; grown for ornament and
perfumery in S.–W. Europe.

## Silver Wattle, Mimosa
*Acacia dealbata*

  ‡

A beautiful, delicate, silvery-
grey evergreen tree with smooth
grey bark. Leaves large, with
10–12 pairs of pinnae each with
30–50 pairs of leaflets 3–4 mm.
Flowers in long branched
clusters, individual heads (1)
about 5 mm. Widely planted
and naturalized in S. Europe.
*A. mearnsii* is similar, but young
twigs and leaves yellowish,
hairy; leaflets only 2 mm.
Planted in S.–W. Europe.

a

b

c

### Sydney Golden Wattle
*Acacia longifolia*

 ‡

Readily distinguished by the slender cylindrical clusters of bright yellow, strongly-smelling flowers arising from the leaf axils. A shrub or small tree with stiff, hairless twigs and light green, blunt leaves up to 15 cm, with 2–4 veins. Pod constricted between seeds, turning brown. Planted for dune stabilization in S.–W. Europe.

### Blackwood Acacia
*Acacia melanoxylon*

 ‡

An erect tree with straight dark brown trunk, dull dark green, slightly curved, lanceolate leaves, and clusters of creamy-white flower heads shorter than the leaves. On young trees both twice-pinnate and entire leaves occur mixed (c) which is un-usual. Pod twisted, reddish-brown seeds with a double-folded red stalk. Planted for timber in S.–W. Europe.

### Blue-Leaved Wattle
*Acacia cyanophylla*

 ‡

A small, slender-branched tree distinguished by its bluish-green, linear to lanceolate, one-veined leaves borne on pendu-lous twigs. Flower heads rela-tively large, 1–1.5 cm across, in short clusters of 2–6. Pods constricted between seeds, glaucous then brownish. Plant-ed for soil stabilization and ornament in S. Europe, parti-cularly in the S.E.

a

b    c

d

## PEA FAMILY

*Acacia retinodes*

A small slender-branched tree
to 10 m with light green, sometimes glaucous, willow-like
leaves, and tiny globular sweet-
scented, pale yellow flower
heads in loose clusters. It may
flower at all times of the year
and will grow in most soils, consequently it is widely planted
for ornament in S. Europe,
particularly along the Mediterranean littoral, and is sometimes naturalized. Twigs usually
brown. Leaves 6–15 cm, blunt
or acute. Flower heads 4–6 mm,
in clusters of 5–10. Pod flattened, not or only slightly constricted between the seeds.
Seeds with a scarlet, double
folded encircling stalk.

a

b

**Golden Wattle** (c)
*Acacia pycnantha*
*Acacia cyclops* (d)

The former is a small tree planted for tanning and ornament.
Leaves curved, one-veined;
twigs glaucous. Flower heads
large 8–10 mm, in long clusters.
The latter is a relatively low
shrub to 3 m, sometimes naturalized on coastal cliffs in Portugal.
Leaves with 3–6 veins. Flower
heads yellow, 4–6 mm, solitary or
2–3. Pod twisted (p. 101); seeds
with red swollen stalk.

c

d

104

## Persian Acacia, Pink Siris
*Albizia julibrissin*

 ‡

A small, graceful, deciduous tree with large, ferny, twice pinnate leaves with numerous small curved leaflets. Flowers distinctive, having a tuft of numerous conspicuous pink stamens. Flower heads many, in umbels, at the ends of branches. Pod flat 8–15 cm. An Asian tree; grown for ornament and shade along boulevards in the south.

## Pagoda Tree, Scholar's Tree
*Sophora japonica*

 ‡

A native tree of E. Asia which is frequently grown for ornament in C. Europe, and is locally naturalized. Distinguished by its pinnate leaves with 7–17 oval-lanceolate, shining dark green leaflets which are glaucous or hairy beneath. Twigs glaucous at first, then green; buds hidden in the swollen base of the leaf stalk in summer. Flowers in conical clusters, creamy-white or pale pink, pea-like, 1–1.5 cm. Pod flat, conspicuously constricted between the seeds, hairless, 5–8 cm. It can be confused with False Acacia (see p. 111), but Pagoda Tree has smaller flowers in erect clusters, no spines, and different bark.

a

b

c

d

×1

×2

105

## PEA FAMILY

### Bean Trefoil
*Anagyris foetida*

A low deciduous bush to 4 m with green twigs and trifoliate leaves. A native shrub of dry slopes and scrub throughout the Mediterranean region. Flowers 18–25 mm, curious in having the standard half the length of the other petals. Pod 10–20 cm, turning cream-coloured, foetid. A poisonous, purgative shrub, particularly its violet or yellow seeds.

### Laburnum, Golden Rain
*Laburnum anagyroides*

A native tree of S.–C. Europe where it grows in woods and thickets usually in the mountains to 2,000 m. Elsewhere a familiar and widely grown ornamental tree which is sometimes naturalized. It is a small erect tree to 7 m, with ascending branches and a narrow often irregular crown, or a shrub. The smooth greenish-brown bark is distinctive. Leaves trifoliate with dull green elliptic leaflets, which are greyish with adpressed silky hairs beneath when young; twigs similarly greyish-green, silky-haired. Flowers bright yellow, often with brown streaks, about 2 cm, in long pendulous clusters 10–30 cm. Pods with adpressed hairs when young but becoming nearly hairless. One of the most poisonous of native trees: all parts are poisonous, but particularly the seeds—no parts should be eaten or even tasted. Cytisine and laburnine are the poisonous substances.

## Alpine Laburnum
*Laburnum alpinum*

Very like the previous species, with a similar distribution in Europe. Flowers smaller, 1.5 cm, more sweet scented and numerous, in longer, more slender clusters, 15–40 cm. Clearly distinguished by its almost hairless leaves, twigs, and pods, and brown seeds. Leaflets glossy green above, light green, not grey-green beneath. Found in sunny rocky places, and mountain woods.

*Calicotome villosa*

*Calicotome spinosa* (e)

These two very similar-looking species of Spiny Brooms are prickly, gorse-like shrubs to 3 m, commonly found in thickets and on dry bushy slopes in the Mediterranean region. The former has a wider distribution. It is distinguished by its flowers in clusters of 2–15, its shaggy-haired or silky-haired pods, and more slender spines. Young twigs, undersides of leaves, and calyx densely silvery or shaggy-haired. Leaves trifoliate.

The latter is found in the W. Mediterranean region from Italy to Spain. Distinguished by the flowers which are mostly solitary, and the pods which are hairless or nearly so. Young twigs sparsely silky-haired, becoming nearly hairless, and spines stouter.

## PEA FAMILY

### Broom
*Cytisus scoparius (Sarothamnus s.)*

### Woolly-Podded Broom (c)
*Cytisus grandiflorus*

The well-known, common
Broom, is found throughout
Europe except in the north.
The numerous large yellow
flowers, with long coiled stigmas, are distinctive, as are the
green, 5-ribbed, switch-like,
often nearly leafless stems.
Leaves mostly trifoliate; leaflets
0.5–2 cm. Flowers 1.5–2 cm;
calyx hairless, two-lipped.
Pods black when ripe, hairless
except on margin.
Several other similar-looking
brooms occur in the Iberian
peninsula, distinguished by
small botanical differences.
Woolly-Podded Broom has
larger flowers 2–2.5 cm, and
pod densely covered with long
white hairs. Leaves all stalkless.
Brooms occur in open sunny,
often sandy or rocky places,
less commonly in wood verges
and thickets.

### White Spanish Broom
*Cytisus multiflorus*

A slender, switch-like shrub to
3 m, with five-angled flexible
twigs which are first silvery-
haired, then hairless. Flowers
small, white, about 1 cm, numerous; calyx silky. Pods small
1.5–2 cm, hairy. Usually found
in heathland shrub, or in open
woods or river banks, in C. and
N.–W. Spain and Portugal.
Other *Cytisus* species may sometimes grow to over 2 m.

Broom

a

b

c

d

e

## Montpellier Broom
*Teline monspessulana (Cytisus m.)*

A leafy, spineless shrub to 3 m,
with trifoliate leaves, axillary
clusters of yellow flowers, and
narrow hairy pods. Leaves
stalked; leaflets ovate, with
spreading hairs. Flowers about
1 cm, standard and wings hairless, keel hairy; calyx hairy.
Thickets and open woods in the
Mediterranean region and
Portugal.

## Mount Etna Broom
*Genista aetnensis*

A small, graceful tree to 5 m, restricted to Sardinia and Sicily.
Branches rush-like, leafless;
flowers numerous, yellow, to
1 cm. Pod rounded, with curved
point.
*G. cinerea* is a switch-like
shrub, one of several brooms
found in S.–W. Europe, growing
to over 2 m. It has silky stems
and pods, and silky yellow
flowers.

b

c

*Lygos sphaerocarpa* (d)
*Lygos monosperma* (e)

There are three native species of
these switch-like shrubs, with
rounded, one-seeded pods. The
former, with small yellow
flowers 5–8 mm, is from Spain
and Portugal.
The latter, one of two white-
flowered species, with flowers
1.5 cm, is from Sicily. The other
white-flowered species, *L.
raetam*, has flowers 1–1.2 cm,
and is found in the S.–W.
Iberian peninsula by the sea.

d

e

## PEA FAMILY

### Spanish Broom
*Spartium junceum*

An erect much-branched switch-like shrub, usually seen without leaves, with terminal clusters of showy, sweet-scented, yellow flowers each 2–2.5 cm. Twigs glaucous-green, flexible; leaves simple, strap-shaped. Pods 5–8 cm, becoming black and hairless. A common shrub of the Mediterranean region and Portugal on dry sunny slopes; occasionally naturalized elsewhere.

### *Petteria ramentacea*

A small, dense, deciduous shrub occasionally growing to over 2 m, found in mountain scrub in Yugoslavia and Albania. Its rather large, stalked, trifoliate leaves and erect, terminal, leaf-less clusters of fragrant yellow flowers distinguish it. Calyx two-lipped, the upper lip deeply divided, the lower three-toothed.

### Gorse
*Ulex europaeus*

An unmistakable, very spiny, dense shrub growing to 3 m, of heaths and grassy places of Western Europe. Naturalized northwards to Scandinavia and eastwards to Austria. Stems, lateral branches, and narrow leaves are all spine-tipped (1). Flowers chrome-yellow, scented, short-stalked, 1.5–2 cm; calyx and bracteoles (3) densely hairy. Pod little longer than the persisting calyx (2).

*Adenocarpus complicatus*

A spineless shrub distinguished by its pods which have conspicuous glandular swellings (1). It is a dense shrub of S.–W. Europe and the Mediterranean region, with stems and leaves usually silvery-haired. Leaflets oblanceolate.
*Adenocarpus decorticans* is more attractive with narrow silvery leaflets about 1 mm wide, and larger flowers, 1.5 cm. Mountains of S. Spain.

*Adenocarpus decorticans*

**Yellow Tree Lupin**
*Lupinus arboreus*

A branched, winter-green shrub to 3 m, native of California, which is naturalized in the British Isles usually near the sea. The palmate leaves (2) with 5–12 leaflets are distinctive. Flowers scented, in terminal spike-like clusters 10–30 cm long; petals usually yellow but may be white, blue, purple or variegated.

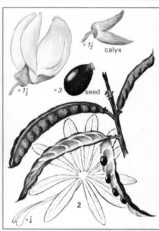

calyx

seed

**False Acacia**
*Robinia pseudacacia*

A native of C. and N. America which has long been introduced to Europe and is now widely naturalized, mainly in the south and west. Mature trees are picturesque, reaching 25 m with rugged, deeply furrowed trunks and twisted, brittle branches bearing light green foliage. It suckers freely and may form dense thickets of young spiny stems. Leaves pinnate with 7–21 oval, hairless leaflets

a

b

c

d

## PEA FAMILY

2.5–4.5 cm, often with spines at their base. Flowers white, numerous in pendulous clusters 10–20 cm, sweet-scented. Pods 5–10 cm, brown, smooth, and hairless. Often planted for stabilizing soil particularly in sandy areas and on embankments. It can be confused with Pagoda Tree—see p. 105.

a

### Chinese Wisteria
*Wisteria sinensis*

  ‡

A robust, deciduous, climbing shrub to 10 m with compound leaves, and long pendulous clusters of deep violet, or mauve flowers. Native of E. Asia; often planted for ornament, and cover, and occasionally locally naturalized. Leaflets 7–13, oval-pointed, silky-haired when young, later hairless. Flowers 2.5 cm, in pendulous clusters 15–20 cm long; pods velvety, 10–15 cm.

b

c

### Bladder Senna
*Colutea arborescens*

A much-branched, erect, thornless shrub to 6 m, with very distinctive inflated bladder-like fruits. Leaves with 9–11 broadly elliptical leaflets. Flowers 1.5–2 cm, yellow, often brown-streaked. Native of S. and S.–C. Europe on dry slopes and open woods.
*C. cilicica* is similar, with larger flowers to 2.2 cm, with wings longer than keel. N. Greece and Turkey.

d

e

## False Indigo
*Amorpha fruticosa*

  ‡

A deciduous shrub of N. America which has become naturalized by streams and waysides in C. and S. Europe. Leaves pinnate with 11–25 oval to elliptic, gland-dotted leaflets. Flowers about 6 mm, blue-purple with conspicuous yellow anthers, in long, dense, erect spikes. Pod curved, 7–9 mm, also gland-dotted (1).

## Tree Medick, Mountain Trefoil
*Medicago arborea*

A compact, semi-evergreen shrub to 4 m, with densely silky-haired twigs and young leaflets, and distinctive flattened, sickle-shaped, or spirally-coiled pods (see p. 99 (8)). Leaves trifoliate; leaflets obovate. Flowers 1–1.5 cm yellow, in short tight clusters. Native of rocky places in the S. Mediterranean region; sometimes naturalized elsewhere.

## SPURGE FAMILY
### Euphorbiaceae
### Castor Oil
*Ricinus communis*

  ‡

Most commonly a robust annual, but in the south it grows into a tree to 4 m. A tropical plant; cultivated for its oily seed, often naturalized in S. and S.–C. Europe. Conspicuous with its very large palmately 5–9-lobed leaves. Flowers one-sexed, reddish. Fruit 1–2 cm, with or without prickles; seed shiny, mottled, with a large swelling.

a

b

c

d

e

1    ×1½    ×1½

# RUE FAMILY                    Rutaceae

This family of about 1,300 species of herbs, trees and shrubs is distinguished by the presence of translucent glands in the leaves which contain strongly aromatic oils as in Rue, Dittany, and *Citrus*. Mostly from the S. temperate regions and tropics; no woody species is native in Europe. The cultivated citrus species, widely grown for their fruits and aromatic oils in orchards and gardens in the Mediterranean region, have all developed from S.–E. Asian species, but their parentage is obscure. They are distinguished by their large fruits with thick leathery rind and juicy pulp. Flowers with 4–5 sepals, usually 5 petals, numerous stamens, and a superior ovary (1).

Seville Orange

## Seville Orange
*Citrus aurantium*

A small, evergreen tree with a rounded crown, spiny twigs, and leaves with rather broadly winged leaf stalks (2). Leaves broadly elliptical 7.5–10 cm. Flowers white, very fragrant, one or several in each leaf axil. Fruit orange, about 7.5 cm, globular, but slightly flattened at both ends, with a rough, bitter rind, and bitter sour flesh. An excellent marmalade orange.

a

## Sweet Orange
*Citrus sinensis*

Very like the previous, but the fruit differs in having nearly smooth rind, and flesh which is sweet when ripe. Leaf stalks narrowly-winged, oblanceolate in outline, (broader, obcordate in Seville Orange). Flowers white, fragrant, in short lax clusters, or solitary. Fruit varying in size, with thick or thin orange-yellow to yellow rind.

b

c

## Tangerine
*Citrus deliciosa*

A small spreading tree with spiny twigs, narrowly elliptic leaves, and distinctive orange fruits. They are 5–7.5 cm across, globular, but distinctly flattened above and below, with a thin, sweetly aromatic, bright orange rind when ripe which easily separates from the sweet flesh. Flowers white, solitary or clustered.

## Citron (c)
*Citrus medica*
## Shaddock, Pomelo (d)
*Citrus grandis*

The former is a small tree with toothed leaves and rounded or narrowly winged leaf stalks, and very large yellow fruit, 15–25 cm. Rind very thick, rough; flesh pale green or yellow, acid or sweetish.
The latter has large yellow fruit 10–25 cm like Grapefruit, but twigs and undersides of midvein of leaves sparsely hairy.

## Grapefruit
*Citrus paradisi*

A small, evergreen tree distinguished by its large pale yellow globular fruit 10–15 cm, with thick, smooth, rind, and pale flesh. Leaves with a very broadly winged leaf stalk, wing up to 1.5 cm at its widest. Flowers white in axillary or terminal clusters. Twigs and undersides of leaves hairless.

a
b
c
d
e

115

## RUE FAMILY

### Lemon
*Citrus limon*

  ‡

Unmistakable when bearing ripe fruit. They are pale yellow, oblong-ovoid with a broad nipple-like swelling at the tip, and the flesh is acid.
Leaf stalk narrowly winged, distinctly jointed; leaf blade toothed. Flowers white, flushed purple outside; stamens very numerous 25–40. Twigs with stout spines.

### Sweet Lime (c)
*Citrus limetta*
### Bergamot Orange (d)
*Citrus bergamia*

  ‡

The former is very like the lemon but the fruit shorter, insipidly sweet, and flowers pure white.
The latter has pale yellow, pear-shaped fruit 7.5–10 cm across, with thin peel and fragrant flesh. It is grown in S. Italy for its rind which is rich in aromatic oils.

### Hop Tree
*Ptelea trifoliata*

A shrub or small spreading tree with trifoliate leaves, dense clusters of greenish-white flowers, and drooping bunches of flattened disk-like fruits. A native of N. America; planted for ornament and sometimes naturalized in C. Europe. Petals and stamens 4, densely hairy. Fruit 1.5–2.5 cm, becoming straw-coloured and conspicuously net-veined.

116

## QUASSIA FAMILY
### Simaroubaceae

**Tree of Heaven**
*Ailanthus altissima*

  ‡

A handsome, rapid growing, deciduous tree with large pinnate leaves, and clusters of strong-smelling greenish flowers. A native of China; widely planted for ornament, shade, and soil conservation, particularly in polluted atmospheres, and widely naturalized in S. and C. Europe. Leaves 45–60 cm, with 13–25 large oval-lanceolate leaflets, each with 2–4 teeth near the base and each tooth with a large gland beneath. Twigs smooth; buds scarlet (1). Flowers 7–8 mm across, with male and female flowers often on different trees. Fruit in large, hanging clusters, reddish-brown when young, each seed with a twisted, propeller-like wing. Bark grey, smooth—like Beech. Due to suckering it often forms thickets of young stems by roadsides and on waste places. A member of a small mostly tropical family of trees and shrubs, the *Simaroubaceae*.

## MAHOGANY FAMILY
### Meliaceae

**Persian Lilac, Bead Tree**
*Melia azedarach*

  ‡

A small, spreading, deciduous tree to 15 m, with twice-pinnate leaves, lilac flowers, and pea-sized, yellow to cream-coloured fruits. A native of S. and E. Asia; widely planted in S. Europe for shade by roadsides and ornament, and locally naturalized. Leaflets numerous,

oval to elliptic, 2–5 cm, sharply toothed or lobed. Flowers in loose branched clusters 10–20 cm across, fragrant. Petals violet, spreading, stamen tube darker violet. Fruit often persisting on bare stems during the winter; they have been used medicinally and are somewhat poisonous—also used as beads! A member of the Mahogany Family, *Meliaceae*, which is largely tropical.

a

b

## CORIARIA FAMILY
### Coriariaceae

**Mediterranean Coriaria, Redoul**

*Coriaria myrtifolia*

A suckering shrub with erect wand-like branches to 3 m, of thickets, hedges and banks in S.–W. Europe. Its petals become fleshy and enclose the fruits. Twigs quadrangular; leaves opposite, three-veined. Flowers tiny, greenish, in short clusters. Fruit five-lobed and ribbed, poisonous.

c

d

## CASHEW FAMILY      Anacardiaceae

A small family of about 600 species which are largely tropical and subtropical. There are 7 native species in Europe. Distinguished by their small regular flowers (1), in branched clusters, with petals and sepals usually 5, and stamens usually 10. Fruit commonly a resinous drupe. Leaves pinnate, palmate, or simple. Most contain an acrid milky juice or are resinous, and in consequence are often valuable as sources of gums and resins, as dye plants, or for tanning leather. Some are poisonous, even to the touch, but none of these is a European species.

Mastic Tree

Wig Tree

Turpentine Tree    ×1½    Sumach    ×3    1

**Sumach** (a)
*Rhus coriaria*
**Staghorn Sumach** (b) ‡
*Rhus typhina*

The former is a hairy, semi-
evergreen shrub to 3 m, with
pinnate leaves (1), dense greenish
flower clusters (a), and
brownish-purple fruit. Leaflets
7–21, coarsely toothed, leaf
stalk winged above.
The latter is often planted for
ornament. Leaf stalk not
winged; fruits crimson,
remaining through winter.

**Wig or Smoke Tree**
*Cotinus coggygria*

A dense spreading shrub, often
only 1–2 m, but growing occasionally to 5 m, with neat
rounded leaves which turn a
brilliant red in autumn. Found
on dry rocky slopes in S.
Europe, excluding the Iberian
peninsula.
Leaves long-stalked, glaucous,
conspicuously veined, 3–8 cm.
Flowers yellowish, in open,
branched, pyramidal clusters;
many are sterile and soon fall
leaving hairy stalks. Fruiting
clusters quite unmistakable
first brown or purplish then
grey with a multitude of stalks
covered with plume-like hairs
(2): the whole appearing as a
'wig', or 'smoke' over the
leaves in summer and autumn.
Fruit 3–4 mm, brown, shining.
The young branches are used
for tanning leather, and the
bark for dyeing. A poisonous
plant.

119

# CASHEW FAMILY

## Terebinth, Turpentine Tree
### *Pistacia terebinthus*

  *

A grey-stemmed deciduous shrub or small tree to 5 m with rather leathery pinnate leaves. Found in open woods, thickets, and dry rocky slopes in the Mediterranean region and Portugal. Leaves (1) with 3–9 ovate to oblong leaflets, with a rounded, not winged rachis (continuation of leaf-stalk). Flowers one-sexed, greenish to reddish-purple (b), in dense clusters, appearing at the same time as the young leaves. Fruit in branched clusters, strikingly coral-red when young (2), but turning brown. The whole plant is resinous.

Large Terebinth, *P. atlantica,* is taller, up to 10–12 m. It has narrower lanceolate leaflets: finely hairy leaf stalk, and narrowly winged rachis. Native of Turkey, reaching N.–E. Greece.

a

b

c

## Mastic Tree, Lentisc
### *Pistacia lentiscus*

  *

A common, usually small spreading, evergreen shrub or sometimes a tree to 8 m of dry stony slopes and thickets of the Mediterranean region and Portugal. Leaves pinnate (3) with 6–12 dark green, leathery lanceolate leaflets (no terminal leaflets), and a broadly winged rachis. Flowers in dense, spike-like clusters. Fruit very aromatic, red then black.

d

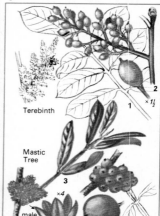

Terebinth

1   2   $\times 1\frac{1}{2}$

Mastic Tree

3   $\times 4$

male flowers   $\times 2\frac{1}{2}$

**Pistachio**
*Pistacia vera*

  ‡

A small deciduous grey-stemmed tree with leaves with 1–3
or more large, grey-green, ovate
leaflets which are at first finely
hairy, but become hairless. The
large fruit about 2.5 cm long
with hard outer shells and
edible seeds are the pistachio
nuts for which the trees are
grown, mainly in the Eastern
Mediterranean region. A native
of Asia.

**Pepper Tree, Peruvian
Mastic Tree**
*Schinus molle*

   ‡

A small, evergreen tree, or
shrub, with pendulous branches
with neat, pinnate, aromatic
leaves. Leaflets 15–27, rachis
not winged. Flowers yellowish-
white; fruit pink. Often planted
for ornament in S. Europe.
*S. terebinthifolia* also from C.
America is locally naturalized in
S.–W. Europe. Fruit bright red.
Leaflets 5–15, rachis winged,
branches not pendulous.

a

b

c

d

# MAPLE FAMILY                Aceraceae

A small family of about 150 species, almost all of the genus
*Acer*, of usually deciduous trees with characteristically palmately-lobed, opposite leaves (3), though leaves sometimes
pinnate or entire. Flowers small, in clusters (1). Sepals, petals,
and stamens usually 8, inserted on a disk (2). Carpels 2; styles 2.
Fruit (4) dividing into 2 winged units, which spin as they fall,
thus facilitating their dispersal. Sap often milky; an American
species produces maple syrup. There are about 13 native European trees and shrubs.

## MAPLE FAMILY

### Key to MAPLES (*Acer*)

1 Leaves pinnate with 3–7 leaflets.    **Box-Elder** (p127)

1 Leaves simple, shallowly or deeply 3–7 lobed, or entire.

   2 Leaves less than 8 cm long, more or less leathery.

     3 Wings of fruit horizontal (8); leaves ciliate.    **Field** (p123)

     3 Wings of fruit more or less parallel (6), or diverging at an acute angle (7).    **Cretan, Montpellier** (p126), **Italian, Balkan** (p125), **Greek** (p124), *granatense* (p125)

   2 Leaves up to 15 cm long, not leathery (1).

     4 Leaves mostly undivided or slightly 3-lobed (3).    **Tatarian** (p124)

     4 Leaves distinctly 3, 5, or 7-lobed (5) (9).

       5 Middle lobe of leaf separated nearly to the base (9).    **Greek** (p124)

       5 Leaf lobed to not more than $\frac{2}{3}$ of the distance to the base (1).

         6 Inflorescence a long pendulous spike-like cluster (2).    **Sycamore** (p124)

         6 Inflorescence a more or less flat-topped, or domed, erect or pendulous cluster (4).

           7 Leaf stalks without milky juice; wings of fruit diverging at an acute angle (7).    **Italian, Balkan** (p124), **Greek** (p124), *granatense* (p125)

           7 Leaf stalks with milky juice; wings of fruit diverging at an obtuse angle, sometimes nearly horizontal.    **Field** (p123), **Norway** (p122), **Lobel's** (p122)

### Norway Maple
*Acer platanoides*

   † *

A handsome, large, spreading tree to 30 m with dense, pale green foliage and very angular lobed leaves with pointed teeth. Found in forests over most of Europe except the extreme north, and occurring only in mountains in the south. Very attractive in spring when the erect, pale yellow flower clusters (4) appear on bare branches before the young leaves

a

open. Terminal buds reddish; opening buds with conspicuous bud scales (2). Leaves with 5 or 7 lobes with central lobes parallel-sided, and several teeth with long thread-like tips; leaf stalks long, with milky juice. Young shoots glaucous. Fruit with wide-spreading to almost horizontal wings (1), spreading 6–10 cm. The timber is pale and hard.

Lobel's Maple *A. lobelii,* native of mountain woods of C. and S. Italy, is similar, but is a columnar tree and has leaf lobes almost without teeth.

## Field Maple
*Acer campestre*

    † *

A shrub or small tree to 20 m, with 3- or 5-lobed, rather thick leaves, and small fruits with horizontal wings (3). A widespread European species reaching as far north as S. Sweden, restricted to mountains in the south. In S.–E. Europe it hybridizes with Montpellier and Cretan Maples making identification sometimes difficult. Leaves variable, divided to about $\frac{1}{2}$ way with mid-lobe parallel-sided at the base, or more deeply cut; lobes blunt, ciliate. The leaves turn golden-yellow to reddish in autumn. Twigs brown; buds and twigs finely hairy. Flowers greenish, appearing with the leaves in erect clusters (4). Fruit finely hairy or hairless, crimson then yellow. Trunk finely fissured with narrow ridges.

# MAPLE FAMILY

## Sycamore
*Acer pseudoplatanus*

  † *

A large spreading tree to 30 m, with sombre foliage, and coarsely 5-lobed leaves cut to about ½ way. Leaf blades dark green above, paler almost glaucous beneath, lobes coarsely toothed; leaf stalks long, without milky juice. Flowers in narrow, pendulous, stalked clusters, 6–12 cm long (1). Fruit with wings usually diverging at a right-angle (2). Bark flaking into shallow irregular plates. Native of S. and C. Europe in woods and hedges, mainly in the mountains; it is widely planted for shelter and ornament further north and is frequently naturalized as in Great Britain. Timber hard, pale, and fine-grained.

a

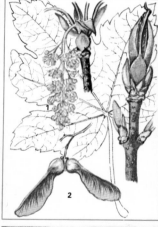

b

## Tatarian Maple (c)
*Acer tataricum*

## Greek Maple (d)
*Acer heldreichii*

The former is distinguished from all others by the un-lobed, or very shallowly 3-lobed leaves (p. 122 (3)). Flowers greenish-yellow, in erect clusters. Wings of fruits almost parallel.
The latter distinctive in having the mid-lobe of the leaf cut nearly to the base (p. 122(9)).

c

d

124

# Italian Maple
## *Acer opalus*

Distinctive in spring with its clusters of long-stalked, pendulous greenish-yellow flowers appearing before or with the young leaves. A small or medium-sized tree to 15 m, or a shrub, found mainly in Italy, France and Spain. The 5-lobed leaves have shallow triangular-acute lobes, they become hairless beneath except on the veins. Fruit with wings diverging at an acute angle (p. 122 (7)).

## *Acer obtusatum*

Very closely related to the previous species but distinguished by its short, wide, blunt leaf lobes and by the undersides of the leaves which remain densely hairy, often woolly beneath. The stalks of the flower clusters are also hairy. A tree of Corsica, Sardinia, Italy, and the Balkan peninsula.

# Balkan Maple (d)
## *Acer hyrcanum*

## *Acer granatense* (e)

The former, like the previous species, has long-stalked pendulous flowers, but different leaves. Lobes deeply cut, parallel-sided, nearly hairless beneath; leaf stalks slender. The latter has similar shaped leaves, but they remain densely hairy beneath. Young twigs and leaf stalks, hairy.

a
b
c
d
e

×2   ×2   ×2   ×2

# MAPLE FAMILY

## Montpellier Maple
### *Acer monspessulanum*

A small deciduous tree or shrub distinguished by its small leathery three-lobed leaves (1). Leaf blades 3–8 cm, dark shiny green above, somewhat glaucous beneath, lobes rarely toothed; leaf stalks reddish. Flowers greenish-yellow, in flat-topped clusters, at first erect then drooping, appearing with or before the leaves. Fruit often flushed pink, with wings that are nearly parallel (2), or sometimes overlapping. It is found in dry hills, thickets, and rocky places throughout southern Europe.

a

b

c

## Cretan Maple
### *Acer sempervirens (orientale)*

An evergreen shrub or small tree of S. Greece and the Aegean region with small undivided or shallowly three-lobed, stiff, leathery leaves, 2–5 cm, hairless and green beneath. Flowers few, greenish-yellow, in erect clusters. Fruit with nearly parallel or acutely diverging wings. It is found on dry rocky hillsides and in thickets. Twigs become spiny when heavily grazed.

d

e

## Box-Elder
*Acer negundo*

  ‡

A native tree of N. America which is frequently planted for ornament and shelter, particularly along roadsides. It is occasionally naturalized in S. and C. Europe. A fast-growing, short-lived tree to 20 m, with green twigs, and trunks often with numerous sprouting shoots. Unlike other maples in having pinnate leaves with 3–5, light green, coarsely and irregularly toothed leaflets. Flowers greenish, appearing before the leaves, the males (b) in erect clusters, the females pendulous. Fruit with narrow, acutely diverging wings, turning pale brown and often remaining on branches long after the leaves.

There are a number of ornamental varieties; the commonest, *Variegatum*, has broad white margins to the leaflets; it often reverts on some branches to the normal green leaves.

a

b

c

d

## SOAPBERRY FAMILY
### Sapindaceae

### China-Tree, Pride of India
*Koelreuteria paniculata*

  ‡

A distinctive, graceful, deciduous tree with large pinnate leaves, pyramidal clusters of small yellow flowers, and inflated bladdery fruits (f). Leaves with 7–15 toothed or lobed leaflets. Flowers about 1 cm across; petals 4; stamens downy. Fruit ovoid, pointed, 4–5 cm. A native of E. Asia; widely planted for ornament in the south.

e

f

## HORSE-CHESTNUT FAMILY
### Hippocastanaceae

**Horse-Chestnut**

*Aesculus hippocastanum*

  † *

A large, striking tree, unlike any other, with its palmate leaves, pyramidal clusters of white flowers, and its spiny fruits containing shiny nuts or 'conkers'. It is found wild only in the Balkan peninsula, but it has been very widely planted for ornament and shade throughout most of Europe (though not in the north), and locally naturalized. A massive tree to 25 m with outcurved branches and dark brown, flaking bark. The large sticky buds and horse-shoe-shaped leaf scars (1) are distinctive. Leaves with 5–7 large, toothed, stalkless leaflets. Flowering spikes 15–30 cm. Fruit inedible, they contain tannins and saponins and are sometimes used in times of shortage.

There are about 25 species in this family.

**Red Horse-Chestnut**

*Aesculus carnea*

  ‡

A tree of garden origin, a hybrid between a N. American Buckeye and Horse-Chestnut, sometimes planted for ornament in Europe. It differs from the latter in its pinkish or red flowers, its non-sticky buds and fruit with few or no prickles, and its dull brown nuts. Leaflets usually 5, 8–15 cm, dark green, somewhat shiny above.

## HOLLY FAMILY
### Aquifoliaceae

**Holly**
*Ilex aquifolium*

  † *

A well-known evergreen shrub
or small tree to 10 m (or more
in cultivation), of woods, thickets, and hedges in S. and W.
Europe. The shiny leathery
leaves usually have spiny
prickles on the undulating
margin (2), though they may be
quite or nearly smooth and
spineless (1), particularly on
older trees. Twigs green or
purplish, hairless; buds minute.
Trees one-sexed; flowers fragrant, about 8 mm across, in
crowded clusters. Fruit bright
red, fleshy, four-seeded, poisonous. Bark smooth, silvery-grey;
timber pale, very dense.
Numerous forms with variegated,
contorted, spiny, or smooth
leaves are grown for ornament.
*I. colchica* reaches Turkey-in-
Europe from further east. It
differs in being a shrub to 3 m,
with spiny leaves which turn
black on drying.

a

b

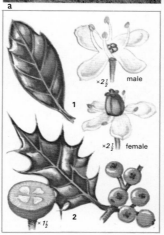

c

## SPINDLE-TREE FAMILY    Celastraceae

A small family of 500 species of trees, shrubs, and climbers
widely distributed in the world; 5 species are native to Europe.
A few are ornamental, but the family is of no economic importance. Botanically it is distinguished by the ovary which has a
fleshy disk often fused to the base of the stamens (4), and fruit
(5) with seeds which are covered by a brightly-coloured coat or
aril. Leaves simple, opposite (3). Flowers white to greenish, in
small flat-topped clusters. Sepals, petals, and stamens 4 or 5.
Ovary with 2–5 cells, each cell with two seeds.

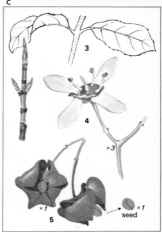

# SPINDLE-TREE FAMILY

## Spindle-Tree
### *Euonymus europaeus*

A small, slender, deciduous tree to 6 m, or a much branched shrub, with smooth green bark and twigs. Widespread throughout Europe except in the extreme north, and the Mediterranean region. Twigs more or less quadrangular; buds green, ovoid (1). Leaves hairless, up to 10 cm, margin finely toothed. Flowers, usually with 4 petals (2), in lateral clusters of 3–8. Fruit (3) deep pink, with 4 rounded, paired, segments which split revealing the seeds, which are covered by an orange-red fleshy coat, or aril. In autumn, its masses of deep pink fruit and rich red foliage make it one of the most attractive woody plants in hedgerows and thickets in the lowlands and hills.

a

b

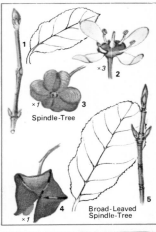

Spindle-Tree

Broad-Leaved Spindle-Tree

## Broad-Leaved Spindle-Tree
### *Euonymus latifolius*

A small tree or shrub similar looking to the previous species, but leaves longer 8–16 cm, and broader to 7 cm, and buds spindle-shaped pointed (5). Flowers usually with 5, more rounded petals; and fruits (4) more angular, usually 5-celled. A plant of woods and thickets of S.–C. and S.–E. Europe, from France eastwards.

c

d

## Rough-Stemmed Spindle-Tree
*Euonymus verrucosus*

A small shrub up to 3 m, of
woods and thickets of E. and
E.–C. Europe, distinguished by
the dark brown warty swellings
on the rounded twigs. Leaves
up to 6 by 3.5 cm, often finely
hairy on the veins beneath.
Flowers solitary or in clusters of
only 2–3. Fruit with 4 rounded
cells; seeds black, only partly
covered by the orange aril.

## Japanese Spindle-Tree
*Euonymus japonicus*

  ‡

A small evergreen tree or shrub
from Japan, with shiny dark
green obovate, toothed leaves.
Widely planted for its dense
compact growth particularly in
S. and W. Europe and sometimes naturalized in the south.
Flowers greenish-yellow (c).
Fruit pinkish, small, with 4
rounded cells. Many cultivated
forms with variegated leaves,
are grown for ornament.

## BLADDERNUT FAMILY
### Staphyleaceae

### Bladdernut
*Staphylea pinnata*

The only European member of a
small family, the *Staphyleaceae*,
with 24 species, of the north
temperate region. It is distinguished by the inflated bladder-
like fruits, which split at the
tips and contain one or a few
seeds. The Bladdernut is a
deciduous shrub to 5 m, with
pinnate leaves, drooping flower
clusters and bladdery fruits. It

131

is native in thickets and woods in C. Europe. Leaflets 5–7, finely toothed, hairless, with pointed scales at the base of each leaflet (p. 131 (1)). Flowers in long clusters 5–12 cm. Fruit 2.5–4 cm; seeds large, yellowish-brown.

## BOX FAMILY
### Buxaceae

**Common Box**
*Buxus sempervirens*

 *

An evergreen shrub or small tree to 5 m with neat oval, glossy dark green leathery leaves, which is widespread and locally abundant on dry hills in S.–W. and W.–C. Europe. Twigs 4-angled. Leaves opposite, 1.5–3 cm, hairless, paler green beneath with somewhat inrolled margins. Flowers without petals, one-sexed, with one female (3) and several male (1) flowers in axillary clusters. Fruit a 3-celled capsule (2) with short, straight persisting styles; seeds glossy black. This is one of two European species of a small mostly tropical family, the *Buxaceae*, distinguished largely by the structure of its ovary.

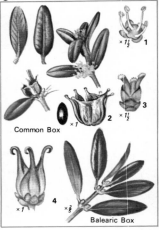

Common Box

Balearic Box

**Balearic Box**
*Buxus balearica*

A rare native small tree or shrub of the Balearic Islands, Sardinia and the S. coast of Spain. Like the previous but more upright, with larger leaves, 2.5–4 cm; larger flower clusters, about 1 cm across; and fruits with persisting curved styles nearly as long as the capsule (p. 132 (4)). The twigs are stouter and the leaves yellow-green and less glossy.

a

b

## BUCKTHORN FAMILY    Rhamnaceae

A cosmopolitan family of about 550 species, with about 6 larger shrubby species or small trees native in Europe. Botanically it is distinguished by its simple unlobed leaves; its perigynous flowers in which the ovary is surrounded at the base by a rim or cup from which the sepals, petals, and stamens arise (1); and its stamens which are placed opposite the petals. Sepals, petals, and stamens usually 4 or 5. Ovary with 2–4 cells, each one-seeded; fruit often fleshy. A family of little economic importance, though some species have been used medicinally and for dyeing; a small number are ornamental.

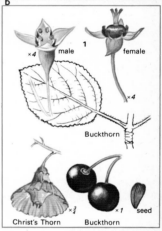

×4   male        female
1
×4

Buckthorn

Christ's Thorn    Buckthorn    seed
×¾    ×1

**Christ's Thorn, Jerusalem Thorn**
*Paliurus spina-christi*

An extremely spiny, clinging, much-branched, erect shrub to 3 m, often found in dense impenetrable clumps in the hotter and drier parts of the Mediterranean region and Balkan peninsula. The flexible, zig-zag, finely hairy twigs have numerous pairs of needle-sharp alternately straight and hooked spines, and two ranks of neat oval, minutely toothed leaves, 2–4 cm. Flowers

c

d

133

yellow, about 2 mm across, in lax axillary clusters. Fruit unmistakable, recalling miniature umbrellas or wide-brimmed hats, with domed crown and spreading undulate wing. Very resistant to grazing, it is sometimes used for boundary hedges in the south.

a

b

### Common Jujube
*Ziziphus jujuba*

Like the previous with its flexible, spiny twigs, but twigs hairless. Fruit (2) different, fleshy and edible, dark reddish-brown to black. Native of Asia; grown for its fruit in the E. Mediterranean region and frequently naturalized.
*Ziziphus lotus* is native of S. Mediterranean region and has grey twigs and globular, dark yellow fruit (1).

### Mediterranean Buckthorn
*Rhamnus alaternus*

An erect, bushy, nearly hairless evergreen shrub to 5 m, of dry stony places and evergreen thickets in the Mediterranean region and Portugal. Leaves alternate (p. 135 (1)), 2–6 cm variable, lanceolate to ovate, acute or blunt, entire or toothed, shining dark green, leathery; twigs minutely downy. Flowers small, yellowish-green, in dense globular clusters. Sepals usually 5; petals absent. Fruit 4–6 mm,

c

d

red then black, in clusters
amongst the leaves; seeds 3. Its
alternate leaves distinguish it
readily from the often similar-
looking *Phillyrea latifolia*,
(see p. 167), which has opposite
leaves.

## Buckthorn
*Rhamnus catharticus*

 ■ *

A widely distributed deciduous
shrub or small tree to 6 m, of
wood verges, hedges, and
thickets found in most of Europe
from S. Scandinavia southwards,
but not in the Mediterranean
region. Leaves opposite, blunt
or notched at apex, finely
toothed, with 2–4 pairs of conspicuous lateral veins. Old
twigs end in spines, and lateral
shoots continue growth; buds
with scales (3). Bark nearly
black on old trees. Flowers (2)
tiny, sweet-scented, one-sexed,
numerous in clusters amongst
the leaves on short shoots;
sepals and petals 4. Berries
globular, 6–10 mm, first green
then black; four-seeded. They
are poisonous.

135

# BUCKTHORN FAMILY

## Alpine Buckthorn
*Rhamnus alpinus*

A deciduous, usually erect shrub to 4 m, found largely on limestone mountains of S. and S.–E. Europe. Leaves all alternate, 4–10 cm, glossy green, finely toothed, broadly elliptic, blunt or fine-pointed, with 7–20 pairs of conspicuous lateral veins. Fruit 4–6 mm, black.

## Alder Buckthorn
*Frangula alnus*

   *

Unlike the Buckthorn, this species has naked buds (1); alternate, entire, not toothed leaves (2); bisexual flowers (3) with 5 petals, sepals, and stamens. An erect, rather slender-branched shrub or small tree to 5 m or more, found in damp woods, hedges, and bogs on acid soils throughout Europe, except the extreme north and much of the Mediterranean. Leaves 2–7 cm, obovate, with 7–9 conspicuous pairs of lateral veins, becoming hairless; leaf stalk about 2 cm. Twigs green, then brown. Flowers tiny, solitary or in clusters. Berries 6–10 mm, at first red, ripening to black.

136

## VINE FAMILY                    Vitaceae

A family of mostly woody climbing plants with branched tend-rils which arise opposite the leaves (1). It comprises about 600 species, widely distributed in the tropics and sub-tropics; only the Grape vine is native in Europe. Leaves alternate, often aris-ing from swollen or jointed nodes, usually palmately-lobed or pinnate. Flowers minute, in branched clusters (2) arising, like the tendrils, opposite the leaves. Sepals, petals, and stamens 5; petals soon falling. Ovary with 2 cells; fruit a berry with 2–4 seeds. A family of little economic importance except for the Grape vine; a few are ornamental.

### Grape Vine
*Vitis vinifera*

  *

Wild Grape vines, ssp. *sylvestris*, are found in S.–E. and S.–C. Europe. They are one-sexed, the male plants having more deeply-lobed leaves than the females. Fruit small, about 6 mm, bluish-black and acid. Culti-vated Grape vines are grown throughout C. and S. Europe. After thousands of years of cultivation their parentage is obscure. American species with increased resistance to 'phyl-loxera', a disease caused by greenfly, are used either as stocks for grafting the Grape vine, for hybridization with it, or as a pure species. The Grape vine is a robust woody climber to 35 cm, but it is often annually pruned into low bushes, on short woody trunks. It has the characteristic lobed leaves, branched tendrils, and clusters of small greenish flowers (2) of the family. Fruit very fleshy, sweet-tasting, vary-ing in colour from green, red, to purple-black; it is the grape, raisin, sultana, of commerce.

a

b

c

137

# VINE FAMILY

## Boston Ivy
### *Parthenocissus triscupidata*

  ‡

A very vigorous climber from China and Japan, able to attach itself by its tendrils to walls, trees, and upright supports. Widely grown for ornament in Europe; locally naturalized. Leaves three-lobed or with three leaflets, rarely entire. Tendrils branched, with adhesive pads at the tips. Flowers greenish, in branched clusters. Fruits blue, bloomed. Autumn colouring brilliant.

## Virginia Creeper
### *Parthenocissus quinquefolia*

   ‡

A tall woody climber able to grow, like the previous species, up walls or trees. It differs in having palmate leaves with usually 5 stalked, oval-elliptic leaflets which are dull green above and somewhat glaucous beneath. Tendrils with 5–8 branches each ending in an adhesive pad. Flowers in clusters opposite the leaves, with tiny reflexed petals. Fruit blue-black (c), globular, about 6 mm, with 2–3 seeds. A native climber of E. America; widely planted for ornament, wall covering and for its vivid red autumn colouring; naturalized locally in C. Europe and Britain.
*P. inserta* is very similar to Virginia Creeper, and is often grown for ornament. It is distinguished by its tendrils which have 3–5 branches without adhesive pads at their tips, and which coil round branches or swell inside cracks for support. Leaflets shining green beneath. A native of America, often naturalized in C. Europe.

a

b

c

d

# LIME FAMILY                    Tiliaceae

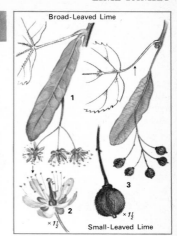
Broad-Leaved Lime

A small family of about 400 trees and shrubs largely restricted to the tropics. Only 4 species of lime are native in Europe. The family is distinguished by the numerous stamens which are in bundles (2), and the branched, flat-topped inflorescence, which in limes have a conspicuous leafy membraneous bract (1), arising from the inflorescence stalk. Petals, sepals 5. Ovary with 5 carpels; fruit with 1–3 seeds. All European limes are interfertile; hybrids are common, and some of these are distinctive and widely planted for ornament; it is consequently often difficult to identify individual trees. The clusters of fruits with their bracts (3), spin in the wind as they fall, facilitating their dispersal.

Small-Leaved Lime

## Key to LIMES (*Tilia*)

1 Leaves white-woolly beneath, with star-shaped hairs (7).    **Silver** (p139), **Weeping Silver** (p139)

1 Leaves finely hairy with simple hairs, or hairless, except on the veins and vein axils beneath (4).

2 Fruit strongly ribbed (5).    **Broad-Leaved** (p141), **Red** (p141)

2 Fruit smooth, or slightly ribbed (6).

3 Inflorescence erect or ascending; cross veins of leaf not prominent.    **Small-Leaved** (p140)

3 Inflorescence pendulous (1); cross veins of leaf prominent.    **European** (p141), **Caucasian** (p142)

**Silver Lime**
*Tilia tomentosa*

**Weeping Silver Lime** (p. 140b)
*Tilia × petiolaris*

A native tree of woods of the Balkan peninsula. Distinguished by its dark leaves, contrasting white-woolly beneath and particularly conspicuous in a wind. A large broadly conical tree, with steeply ascending branches, to 30 m, with white-woolly young twigs. Leaves 8–10 cm, rounded

a                                        b

heart-shaped, toothed or shallowly lobed; leaf stalk about
half as long as the blade.
Flowers dull white, with some
sterile stamens present; in
clusters of 6–10; bract narrow,
blade-like. Fruit 6–8 mm, ovoid,
minutely warty.
The latter is a frequently planted
hybrid, with long pendulous
branches and long slender leaf
stalks, about as long as the
blade, and spathulate bracts to
the inflorescence. Fruit with 5
furrows, nearly always sterile.

## Small-Leaved Lime
*Tilia cordata*

  *

A large domed tree to 30 m,
which is widespread in woods
throughout Europe, except
in the extreme north. It is also
widely planted as a shade and
wayside tree. Distinguished by
its neat heart-shaped leathery
leaves 3–9 cm, which are smaller
than most limes, and which are
pale and hairless beneath except
for reddish-brown tufts of
hairs in the vein-axils (1).
(This distinguishes it from
Broad-Leaved Lime.) Flower
clusters, with 4–15 flowers,
erect or ascending (2), fruits
smooth or obscurely ribbed (3).
Twigs hairless, reddish on the
upper side, greenish beneath;
buds ovoid, shining dark
reddish. Bark at first very
smooth, grey, becoming dark
grey or brown and cracked into
plates.

a

b

c

d

e

140

## Broad-Leaved Lime
### *Tilia platyphyllos*

  † *

Distinguished by its strongly 5-ribbed mature fruits (1) which are usually in clusters of three. A large, shapely, domed tree with numerous steeply ascending branches, to 40 m. It is native of C. and S. Europe, and is often planted for ornament. Leaves and the young twigs show considerable variation in hairiness; leaf blades soft, dark green above, paler beneath, finely hairy on both surfaces, or only beneath (2), or rarely almost hairless beneath; leaf stalk usually hairy. Flowers yellowish-white; bracts 5–12 cm.

Red Lime, *T. rubra*, is like the Broad-Leaved Lime but the leaves are hairless or nearly so, firmer in texture, and have bristle-like teeth on the margins. A tree of S.–E. Europe.

## European or Common Lime
### *Tilia × vulgaris (europaea)*

   † *

A hybrid between the Small-Leaved and Broad-Leaved Limes, sometimes occurring in the wild. Often planted for shade and ornament especially in N.–W. Europe. Many characters are intermediate between the parent trees, but it can usually be distinguished by its densely suckering habit, its hairless leaves, except for white hair tufts in the vein axils beneath (3). Also by its pendulous clusters with

141

## LIME FAMILY

5–10 flowers, and its globular to broadly ovoid fruits which are only slightly ribbed. Trunk with many bosses and sprouts. In summer often blackened and disfigured by a sooty-mould. Caucasian Lime, *T.* × *euchlora*, another hybrid, is often planted in place of the former as it is less susceptible to greenfly and sooty-mould. Leaves long-stalked, dark lustrous green above, with reddish-brown hairs in the vein axils beneath. Flowers 3–7; fruit tapered at both ends.

a

## MALLOW FAMILY
### Malvaceae

**Syrian Ketmia**
*Hibiscus syriacus*

A distinctive deciduous shrub to 3 m with large lilac or white trumpet-shaped flowers with deep purple or reddish centres. Leaves 4–7 cm, three-lobed, with star-shaped hairs beneath. Native of S. and E. Asia; widely grown for ornament and hedges in S. Europe. Many cultivated forms are planted showing a wide range of colour variations.

b

c

## OLEASTER FAMILY    Elaeagnaceae

A small family of about 45 species largely of the northern hemisphere; only the Sea Buckthorn is native in Europe. The family is readily distinguished by the unique silvery or golden-brown scales or star-shaped hairs (4), which cover most of the plant, including the flowers and fruits. Flowers tubular (1), with 2 or 4 lobes; petals absent; stamens 2 or 4. Ovary at the base of a tube (2), which in fruit becomes swollen and fleshy and encloses the seeds. The fruit (5) is consequently berry-like. The family is of little value economically; some species are ornamental and planted in Europe.

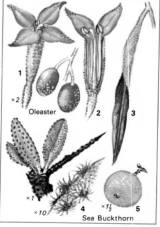

1

×2    Oleaster    2    3

×1

×10    ×1½    5
Sea Buckthorn

## Sea Buckthorn
*Hippophae rhamnoides*

A densely branched spiny
shrub or small tree to 11 m,
which suckers freely and forms
small thickets. It grows by the
sea, on sand-dunes, cliffs, and
along dry river beds and inland
valleys, mainly in the mountains
throughout much of Europe.
Also often planted for soil
stabilization and for ornament,
and naturalized from these
plantings. Leaves 1–6 cm, with
silver or rusty-brown scales
(p. 142 (4)) becoming nearly
scale-less; twigs covered with
scales, spine-tipped. Flowers
greenish, tiny, one-sexed, covered with rust-coloured scales;
appearing in dense clusters in
the female, and short spikes in
the male, before the leaves on
last year's twigs. Fruit (p. 142
(5)) orange, very acid, 6–8 mm.

a

b

c

## Oleaster
*Elaeagnus angustifolia*

A small graceful tree to 7 m or
a spiny shrub, with greyish
willow-like leaves (p. 142 (3))
covered with silvery scales on
the undersides. Native of Asia;
often planted for ornament and
for its edible fruit in S. Europe.
Twigs covered with silvery
scales. Flowers (p. 142 (1))
yellow, fragrant, solitary or in
clusters, about 1 cm long. Fruit
1–2 cm, fleshy, ellipsoid, with
silvery scales.

d

e

143

# ROCKROSE FAMILY    Cistaceae

A family of about 175 species of herbs and small usually ever-green shrubs of the warmer parts of the northern hemisphere, with a considerable concentration in the Mediterranean region. The majority of the shrubby species do not grow as high as 2 m and are consequently excluded. Leaves simple, usually opposite. Flowers regular, with 3–5 sepals, 5 petals, and numerous stamens. Ovary with 3–10 cells; fruit a capsule (1) splitting from above and partly encircled by the persisting sepals. Charac-teristically plants of dry, sunny, rocky places and scrub.

1

flower bud    fruit

**Gum Cistus**
*Cistus ladanifer*

The tallest of the native Euro-pean cistuses, which, in the wild, may grow to 3 m. Foliage very sticky with an aromatic balsam-like smell. Leaves ever-green, green above, white-woolly beneath. Flowers 7–10 cm, pure white or with a crimson centre; sepals 3. Fruit with 10 cells. Forming thickets on dry hills in S.–W. Europe.

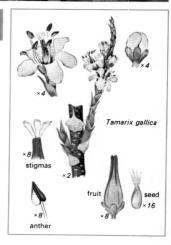

a

# TAMARISK FAMILY    Tamaricaceae

×4

×4

×8
stigmas

×2

*Tamarix gallica*

fruit

seed
×16

×8
anther

×8

A family of very distinctive heath-like shrubs or small feathery trees with slender whip-like branches covered with alternate, tiny scale-like leaves. There are about 100 species, mostly occur-ring in the Mediterranean and C. Asian region. Usually plants of coasts, salt-marshes, sand-dunes, but also of river beds, banks, and salt-rich soils inland. The tamarisks are difficult to identify; they are distinguished from each other by small differences and combinations of characters and they are very similar in general appearance. 9 species are native in Europe, excluding several more from S.–W. Russia. Flowers tiny, usually pink, in clusters. Sepals and petals 4–5; stamens 4 to numerous. Fruit a capsule; seeds with numerous long hairs.

144

*Tamarix smyrnensis*

*Tamarix africana* (c)

A shrub or small tree with reddish-brown bark. Flowers in clusters which are naked at the base; petals 5, very pale pink, rounded or ovate, distinctly keeled. Coastal marshes and mountain streams in E. Balkans and Aegean region.

The latter is found in salt marshes and on river banks in S.–W. Europe, and is sometimes planted for ornament. A tree with black or purple bark, and slender flower clusters 3–6 cm long by 3–8 mm wide, flowering in spring usually before the leaves, or in the autumn. Petals 5, pink or white, 2–3 mm long, persisting. Bracts triangular usually longer than calyx.

*T. tetrandra* is distinguished by its black bark and white flowers mostly with 4 petals. Bracts, the upper part green, longer than the flower stalks, not exceeding the sepals. Usually a spring flowering tree or shrub; mainly of the mountains of E. Balkan peninsula.

*Tamarix gallica (anglica)*

A quite hairless shrub with brown to dark purple branches and lax slender clusters 3–5 mm wide of pink flowers, usually appearing in the summer. Petals 5, 1.5–2 mm long (p. 144).

*T. parviflora*, a native of the Balkan peninsula widely cultivated for ornament in S. and C. Europe, has pale pink, slender flowering spikes 3–5 mm wide; petals 4. Twigs dark purple; bracts papery.

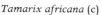

145

## TAMARISK FAMILY

### German Tamarisk
*Myricaria germanica*

A glaucous heath-like shrub to
2.5 m, with wand-like branches
bearing dense elongated terminal clusters of pink flowers and
later fluffy-seeded fruits. Very
like Tamarisk, but differing
botanically by its stamens
which are fused at the base and
by the stalked hair-tufts of the
seeds. An inland plant of river-
gravels and stony places mainly
in C. Europe and Scandinavia.

## CACTUS FAMILY
### Cactaceae

### Prickly Pear, Barbary Fig
*Opuntia ficus-indica*

The commonest of several 'cacti'
which have become naturalized
in the Mediterranean
region. Often planted for
hedges and boundaries and producing an impenetrable barrier;
it is also planted for its edible
fruits. It has an ascending
often tree-like growth to
5 m, with a rounded trunk and
large racket-shaped, oval to
oblong stem joints 20–50 cm,
and no leaves. Joints with scattered bosses from which arise
many small, yellow, barbed
spines, and often 1 or 2
longer, pale spines to 5 cm, but
these may be absent. Flowers
large 7–10 cm, bright yellow,
with numerous petals and
numerous stamens with yellow
filaments. Fruit 5–9 cm, ovoid,
yellow, red or purple, sweet
tasting.
The Cactus family with its
succulent, spiny plants and
showy flowers is native of the
American continent.

a

b

c

*Opuntia maxima (amyclaea)*

  ‡

More tree-like in form than the previous species, to 3 m. Stem joints dull green, with clusters of 1–4 straight white or translucent spines 3 cm long, and short brown spines. Flowers yellow; fruit yellowish-red. *O. monacantha* has bright green joints, with 1–2 yellow to dark reddish spines to 4 cm, arising from felty bosses. Flowers golden yellow; filaments greenish. Fruit reddish-purple. Both are rarely naturalized in the south.

## MYRTLE FAMILY
### Myrtaceae

**Myrtle**
*Myrtus communis*

 *

The only European member of an important tropical family, the *Myrtaceae*, of about 3,000 species which have characteristically leathery, gland-dotted leaves. The Myrtle is widespread in the Mediterranean region and Portugal, where it grows on dry sunny slopes, in pine woods and evergreen thickets. It is widely grown for ornament outside this area. A dense, much-branched evergreen shrub to 5 m, with small, opposite, leathery, gland-dotted, oval-lanceolate leaves (1) which are very aromatic when crushed. Flowers white, sweet-scented, with numerous projecting stamens, long stalked, arising from the axils of the upper leaves. Sepals and petals 5. Ripe fruits bloomed, 7–10 mm long. A famous plant in antiquity.

147

## MYRTLE FAMILY

### Key to GUMS (*Eucalyptus*)

A few of the 300 or so species of Gums native to Australia and Tasmania have been planted in S. Europe. Juvenile and adult leaves are usually very different. Petals and sepals are united to form a cap, the *operculum*, which splits off transversely revealing the numerous stamens. Most commonly planted are:

1 Flowers solitary; fruit more than 1 cm long.     **Tasmanian Blue Gum** (p148)

1 Flowers in umbels (2); fruit not more than 1 cm long.

   2 Individual fruit stalkless (3) or almost so.

     3 Flowers and fruits in umbels of 3; umbel-stalks rounded in section.    **Manna Gum** (p149)

     3 Flowers and fruits usually in umbels of 5–10; umbel-stalks compressed.

       4 Leaves more than 18 cm; bark smooth; fruit glaucous (3).    *maidenii* (p149)

       4 Leaves less than 18 cm; bark fibrous; fruit not glaucous.

         5 Umbel-stalks 7–10 mm; fruit 7–9 by 9 mm, cylindrical.    *botryoides* (p149)

         5 Umbel-stalks 2.5–3.5 cm; fruit 13–20 by 11–15 mm, bell-shaped.    *gomphocephalus* (p150)

   2 Individual fruit distinctly stalked (1).

     6 Umbel-stalks compressed, angular, or strap-shaped.    *resinifer* (p150), **Swamp-Mahogany** (p150)

     6 Umbel-stalks rounded in section, or nearly so.    **Red Gum** (p150), *tereticornis* (p150)

cap

Red Gum

*E. gomphocephalus*

*E. maidenii*

Swamp-Mahogany    Manna Gum

### Tasmanian Blue Gum

*Eucalyptus globulus*

  ‡

Probably the most widely planted gum in the Mediterranean region. A tall, handsome tree to 40 m, with smooth greyish bark exposed by the annual shedding of the outer bark. Mature leaves glossy-green, lanceolate, straight or curved, 10–30 cm by 3–4 cm; young leaves much smaller, oval-heart-shaped, very glaucous. Flowers solitary, whitish, about 4 cm across; cap of flower buds

a

b

148

beaked. Fruit stalkless, globular, flat-topped, large, 1–1.5 cm long by 1.5–3 cm across, with 4 ribs. Often planted in malarial districts and thought to reduce the incidence of the disease by restricting the breeding of malarial mosquitoes. The timber is useful and the leaves of this species yield oil of Eucalyptus.

a

**Manna or Ribbon Gum**
*Eucalyptus viminalis*

 ‡

A large tree to 50 m with white bark with outer bark often hanging in long ribbons. Young leaves (c) clasping stem, mature leaves pale green, lanceolate long-pointed, 11–18 cm by 1.5–2 cm. Flowers red; umbels three-flowered (p. 148 (5)); umbel-stalk rounded, 3–6 mm; bud cap rounded. Fruit 5–6 mm by 7–8 mm, spherical or slightly tapered, valves longer, spreading.

*Eucalyptus maidenii*

 ‡

A large tree to 40 m, with smooth white bark beneath outer deciduous bark. Mature leaves glossy-green, to 20 cm by 2–2.5 cm. Umbels usually 3–7-flowered, borne on stalks 1–1.5 cm which are compressed from side to side. Fruit top-shaped, glaucous (p. 148 (3)).
*E. botryoides* has a hemispherical cap to the flower buds and smaller barrel-shaped fruits 7–9 mm long and wide. Both are planted from Italy westwards.

b

c

d

e

## MYRTLE FAMILY

*Eucalyptus resinifer*

A large tree with reddish bark with rough, persisting fibres. Mature leaves 10–15 cm by 2–3 cm, lanceolate. Umbels with 5–10 yellow flowers; umbel-stalk compressed or angular, 1.5–2 cm. Bud cap pointed, conical. Ripe fruit 5–8 mm long, hemi-spherical.

*E. gomphocephalus* has grey bark; long strap-shaped flower stalks; hemispherical bud cap and bell-shaped fruit 13–20 mm by 11–15 mm (p. 148 (2)).

### Swamp-Mahogany

*Eucalyptus robustus*

A medium sized tree with rough brown persistent bark. Mature leaves (d) broadly lanceolate, 10–18 cm by 4–8 cm. Flowers red, in umbels of 5–10; umbel-stalk strap-shaped 2–3 cm (p. 148 (4)). Bud cap beaked. Fruit cylindrical 12–15 mm with valves much shorter than the rim. Planted in swamps and salty marshes from Italy westwards.

### Red Gum

*Eucalyptus camaldulensis (rostratus)*

A spreading tree with smooth white deciduous bark. Mature leaves linear-lanceolate, 12–22 cm by 0.8–1.5 cm. Flowers red, in clusters of 5–10, on rounded umbel-stalks 1–1.5 cm. Bud cap conical or beaked (p. 148 (1)). Fruit small, hemispherical, 7–8 mm, with valves longer than rim. *E. tereticornis (umbellatus)* has umbel-stalks 5–12 mm: and top-shaped fruit.

a

b

c

d

e

f

## POMEGRANATE FAMILY
### Punicaceae

**Pomegranate**
*Punica granatum*

 ‡ *

A well-known southern shrub
with its crinkled scarlet flowers
and large, golden-red fruit with
juicy orange-like flesh. A native
of S.–W. Asia which is often
grown for its fruit in S. Europe
and widely naturalized in the
Mediterranean region. It is
one of two species of a unique
family, the *Punicaceae*, distinguished by the crown of persistent calyx on the fruit (1).
The Pomegranate is a spiny
deciduous much branched
shrub, or small spineless tree to
5 m. Leaves opposite, 2–8 cm,
shining, hairless; twigs angled,
hairless. Flowers 3–4 cm across
with large reddish, fleshy calyx
tube; petals 4, or more in
double forms; stamens numerous. Fruit globular 5–8 cm;
flesh purple to white, sweet or
acid; seeds numerous. A plant
with many classical associations
and formerly used medicinally.

a

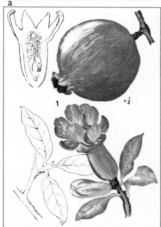

1   $\times\frac{1}{4}$

b

## WILLOW-HERB FAMILY
### Onagraceae

**Fuchsia**
*Fuchsia magellanica*

 ‡

A S. American, cinnamon-brown
stemmed shrub to 3 m, with
unmistakable flowers. It is
naturalized in hedges in W.
Britain and Ireland. Leaves
opposite or in threes, toothed.
Flowers with red calyx tube
and thick red spreading lobes,
broader, shorter violet petals,
and long-projecting stamens
and style. Fruit a black berry.

c

## DOGWOOD FAMILY                    Cornaceae

A small family of about 90 trees and shrubs of tropical and
temperate regions, with only 2 woody species native to Europe.
The family is distinguished from the closely related Umbellifer
Family by the woody habit, fleshy fruit, and leaves usually
opposite. Sepals, petals, and stamens 4 or 5. A family of no
economic importance; a few are grown for ornament and have
occasionally become naturalized in Europe.

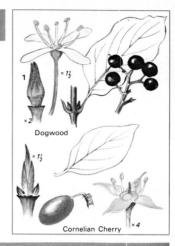

Dogwood

Cornelian Cherry

### Dogwood
*Cornus sanguinea*

A well-known shrub found
throughout Europe, except in
the far north, in scrub, wood
verges, and hedges. It is a
deciduous suckering shrub to
4 m often forming thickets,
with slender, dark red twigs
which are very conspicuous in
winter. Leaves opposite, entire,
4–10 cm, with conspicuous
curved lateral veins, pale green,
turning dark red-purple in the
autumn. Buds without scales (1).
Flowers numerous, in umbels
4–5 cm across, borne at the tips
of the branches; petals 4, narrow, wide-spreading. Fruit
shining black, bitter, in dense
clusters. A colonizer of old
grasslands particularly in alkaline and neutral soils.

a

b

c

## Red-Barked Dogwood (a)
*Cornus alba*
*Cornus sericea (stolonifera)* (b)

The first is a native of Siberia, with dark red, non-suckering, winter shoots. Fruit white, fleshy, with ellipsoid nuts. The second has numerous dark red suckering shoots and forms dense thickets. Very similar to the former but nuts rounded at base. Native of America. Both are naturalized in N. and N.–C. Europe, the latter more commonly so.

## Cornelian Cherry
*Cornus mas*

A small deciduous tree to 8 m, or a shrub, with small clusters of yellow flowers appearing early in the year on bare twigs. A widely distributed native of C. and S.–E. Europe; also planted for ornament and its edible fruit. Leaves opposite, oval to elliptic with 3–5 pairs of conspicuous veins, margins not toothed. Twigs greyish. Flower clusters only 1 cm across, with 10–25 flowers, short-stalked and with 4 yellowish bracts at the base of the cluster. Fruit ovoid, 1.5 cm long, pendulous, fleshy, becoming bright red when ripe. Found on banks, in thickets, and wood verges, usually on calcareous soils.

a

b

c

d

## DOGWOOD FAMILY

### Spotted or Dog Laurel
*Aucuba japonica*

  ‡

A distinctive, dense, evergreen laurel-like shrub growing to 3 m, which is often mistaken for Common or Cherry Laurel. A native of E. Asia; frequently planted for ornament, — particularly the yellow-spotted form —in the west, and sometimes locally naturalized. Bushes one-sexed, the male flower clusters (a) larger, 5–10 cm, than the female. Twigs green, hairless. Fruit scarlet, in clusters.

## IVY FAMILY
### Araliaceae

### Ivy
*Hedera helix*

A very well-known evergreen climber with characteristic dark leathery, lobed leaves, and stout stems covered with brown rootlets by means of which it attaches itself to vertical supports. It is found throughout Europe except in the extreme north, climbing up cliffs, walls and trees, or spreading over the ground in woods and shady places. The leaves are very variable: on shoots in full sun they are elliptical and unlobed (1), on shaded shoots they are deeply or shallowly 3–5-lobed (2)(3). It flowers in late autumn and the spherical greenish umbels are much visited by flies and wasps for the rich supply of nectar. Fruit green then black, 6–8 mm. The only native European member of the Ivy family, *Araliaceae*; a family of 500 species of both tropical and temperate regions.

a

b

c

d

e

**Persian Ivy**
*Hedera colchica*

Growing and looking like the previous species but with very large, scarcely lobed leaves 15–20 cm long, borne on the non-flowering shoots. Hairs on young shoots and inflorescence yellowish-brown, with 15–25 minute rays (6–16 rays on Ivy). A robust climber; native of Turkey and the Caucasus; planted for ornament and sometimes naturalized in S. and W. Europe.

a

## UMBELLIFER FAMILY
### Umbelliferae

**Shrubby Hare's-Ear**
*Bupleurum fruticosum*

One of the few woody European species of the Umbellifer family. A rather straggling evergreen shrub, with neat, erect, rather fleshy glaucous leaves, purplish-green stems, and small compound umbels (1) of numerous yellow flowers. A shrub to 2.5 m of rocky ground and stony places in S. Europe; sometimes planted for ornament.

b

## HEATHER FAMILY          Ericaceae

An important family, particularly in the Mediterranean region and W. Europe where heathlands, moors, and sometimes maquis may be dominated by its members. There are about 1,900 species; 43 are native in Europe. Characterized by their tubular, or bell-shaped flowers with 4–5-lobed corolla. Sepals 4–5; stamens 8–10 with the anthers opening by pores; ovary with 4–5 cells. Fruit either a capsule or, less commonly, a berry. The heathers have needle-like leaves; there are 18 European species, but only a few grow to over 2 m in the wild. Rhododendrons and Strawberry Trees and Wortleberries have broader, often evergreen leaves. Many members of the family are ornamental and are planted; some are naturalized.

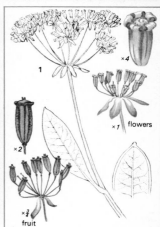

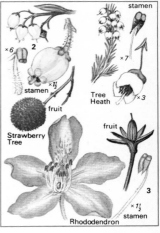

# HEATHER FAMILY

### Tree Heath
*Erica arborea*

### Lusitanian Heath (c)
*Erica lusitanica*

A striking, dense, feathery-looking, evergreen shrub of the Mediterranean region and S.–W. Europe. It often grows up to 4 m and may sometimes become a small tree to 7 m, and is found in open woods, evergreen thickets, on banks, and by streams. Leaves 3–5 mm, needle-like, closely covering the white-haired twigs, usually in whorls of 4. Flowers produced in great numbers, in lateral spike-like clusters. Corolla (3) 2–4 mm long, white, broadly bell-shaped with short lobes and with the darker reddish-purple anthers included within it; stigma white.

The latter is very similar, growing up to 3.5 m. Distinguished by its pink buds, its pale pinkish, longer more cylindrical corolla (2), 4–5 mm, and red stigma. Flowers fragrant.

### Green Heather
*Erica scoparia*

The heather with the smallest and most insignificant flower of all. Corolla (1) bell-shaped, 1–3 mm long, green or variously red-tinged. A slender erect shrub to 6 m, with needle-leaves, 4–7 mm, in whorls of 3–4; found in heaths and open woods in S.–W. Europe eastwards to Italy.

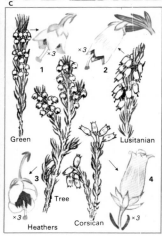

## Corsican Heath
*Erica terminalis*

A shrub of the Mediterranean region of Spain, Corsica, and S. Italy growing to 2.5 m, found in damp ravines, river banks and shady places. Distinguished by its flowers which are in dense terminal umbels of 3–8, and its bright pink urn-shaped corollas (p. 156 (4)) 5–7 mm long, with recurved lobes. Anthers not exposed. Leaves spreading, usually in whorls of 4.

## Rhododendron
*Rhododendron ponticum*

This well-known dark ever-green shrub is often grown for ornament and shelter in the west and is widely naturalized. A rare native of the S.–W. and S.–E. extremes of Europe, by streams and in woods. Leaves leathery, laurel-like, dark, glossy-green, paler beneath. Flowers mauve to lilac-pink, in handsome clusters about 12 cm across. Stamens 10, curved and forward-projecting (p. 155 (3)).

*Rhododendron luteum (Azalea)*

A deciduous shrub of Turkey and further east which reaches S.–E. Europe naturally, though it is rare. A well-known, sweet-scented ornamental shrub, with terminal clusters of yellow flowers appearing on bare twigs before the leaves. Flowers 5 cm across; stamens 5. Leaves oblong-lanceolate, finely toothed, ciliate; buds and shoots sticky. Freely suckering and forming clumps.

## HEATHER FAMILY

**Strawberry Tree**
*Arbutus unedo*

  *

A dense, dark green, evergreen
shrub or small tree to 12 m, of
the Mediterranean region and
S. and S.–W. Europe extending
as far north as S.–W. Ireland. It
is found in evergreen thickets,
wood verges, and dry rocky
slopes. Leaves shining, 4–11 cm,
oblong-lanceolate, usually
with saw-toothed margins; leaf
stalk pinkish, hairy. Young
twigs glandular-hairy, pinkish.
Flowers urn-shaped (p. 155 (2)),
in short pendulous clusters,
white often tinged green or
pink, appearing in autumn
at the same time as the ripe
fruit. Fruit fleshy, with granular
surface, about 2 cm across,
yellow turning to deep crimson,
acid except when fully ripe.
Bark dark brown, shredding in
strips.

a

b

c

**Greek Strawberry Tree**
*Arbutus andrachne*

  †

**Caucasian Whortleberry**
(p. 159b)
*Vaccinium arctostaphylos*

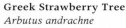

The first is a shrub or small tree
of the E. Mediterranean region.
Like the previous species but
differing in having an orange-
red trunk with peeling bark
which reveals a smooth pale
cinnamon underbark; young
twigs hairless. The flowers

d

e

appear in spring, in erect clusters. Leaves usually not toothed and broader (less than twice as long as wide) than in Strawberry Tree. Fruit small, orange 8–12 mm.

The second is a deciduous shrub or small tree to 5 m restricted to S.–E. Bulgaria and Turkey, found in wooded ravines. Leaves elliptic, finely toothed, richly coloured in autumn. Flowers greenish-white tinged pink, bell-shaped, 5–7 mm, in pendulous clusters of 5–8. Fruit (b) 6–8 mm.

## EBONY FAMILY
### Ebenaceae

**Date-Plum**
*Diospyros lotus*

A small deciduous tree from Asia; often cultivated for its edible fruits in the south. Trees one-sexed. Leaves elliptic, pointed, becoming nearly hairless. Flowers small, stalkless, reddish or greenish-white, bell-shaped with ciliate lobes. Fruit 1.5–2 cm, yellow or bloomed dark purple, with persistent calyx.

**Chinese Persimmon**
*Diospyros kaki*

A small tree from Japan and Korea which is sometimes grown for its large edible fruits in the south. Leaves dark lustrous green above, paler, hairy, beneath. Twigs with brownish hairs. Flowers yellowish-white. Fruit large, tomato-shaped, depressed globular, bright yellow to orange, 3.5–7 cm, extremely astringent when unripe.

## STORAX FAMILY
### Styraceae

**Storax**
*Styrax officinalis*

A rather slender-branched shrub or small deciduous tree to 7 m, with drooping clusters of relatively large white flowers to 2 cm. Leaves and twigs covered with white star-shaped hairs. Fruit a dry drupe. The source of the aromatic gum 'storax'.

a

## OLIVE FAMILY                    Oleaceae

A family of trees and shrubs, rarely climbers, with usually opposite, hairless, simple or compound leaves. It consists of about 500 species, largely found in the temperate and northern tropical regions; 13 are native in Europe. Distinguished by their flowers with characteristically 2 stamens; by their bell-shaped calyx and often tubular corolla; and by the superior two-celled ovary (1), each cell usually with two ovules. Fruit of several types: a berry in privet; a drupe in olive, a capsule in lilac, and a winged fruit in ash. Of some economic importance, particularly because of the olive as a source of oil, and the ashes for timber; many are ornamental and have been introduced into Europe.

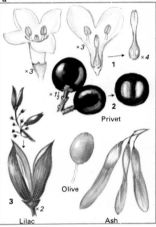

Privet

Olive

Lilac                    Ash

**Key to OLIVE Family**

| | OLEACEAE |
|---|---|
| 1 Leaves compound (5). | **Ashes** (p161–3), **Jasmines** (p163–4) |
| 1 Leaves simple (4) (6). | |
| 2 Leaves covered with small scales beneath. | **Olive** (p166) |
| 2 Leaves not scaly beneath. | |
| 3 Flowers yellow (9). | *Forsythia* (p164) |
| 3 Flowers whitish or lilac. | |
| 4 Flowers inconspicuous, about 2 mm long (8). | *Phillyrea* (p167) |
| 4 Flowers conspicuous, at least 5 mm long. | |
| 5 Flowers lilac (7); fruit dry, splitting (3). | **Lilacs** (p164) |
| 5 Flowers white (1); fruit fleshy (2). | **Privets** (p165–6) |

## Common Ash
*Fraxinus excelsior*

  † *

A well-known and widespread deciduous European tree with a slender grey furrowed trunk, pale green compound leaves, and winged fruit. It is a forest-forming tree to 40 m, growing on deeper soils almost throughout Europe to about latitude 64° N., but not in the Mediterranean region. Distinguished by its sooty-black winter buds (1), and smooth grey twigs. Leaves usually with 7–15 stalkless, broad or narrow, long-pointed leaflets, usually with toothed margins and shaggy hairs on the mid-vein beneath. Flowers purplish in small clusters (4), appearing before the leaves, either male (3) or female, or hermaphrodite (6); petals and sepals absent. Fruit winged (2), 2.5–5 cm long, lanceolate or broader towards the tip. The timber is pale, hard and elastic, and much in demand.

## Narrow-Leaved Ash
*Fraxinus angustifolia*

A smaller tree than the preceding, to 25 m, very like it in many respects, but readily distinguished by its smaller coffee-brown buds (5). Leaflets usually narrower, 8–25 mm wide, oblong to linear-lanceolate, with jagged marginal teeth usually as many as the lateral veins (teeth usually more numerous than lateral veins in Common Ash). Leaflets either hairless beneath, ssp. *angustifolia* (p. 162 (b)),

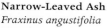

## OLIVE FAMILY

or hairy along the mid-vein beneath towards the base, ssp. *oxycarpa* (a), known as Caucasian Ash. Leaves of young trees with much broader leaflets than adult trees. Fruit 2–4.5 cm, hairless. Trunk soon becoming finely fissured, vertically cracked, and in time knobby. A tree of river banks, or flood-plains and in deciduous forests in S. and S.–E. Europe as far north as Czechoslovakia and Hungary.

*Fraxinus pallisiae*

An uncommon tree of river banks and flood-plains of S.–E. Europe from Romania and Bulgaria eastwards. Very like Narrow-Leaved Ash but with twigs and leaf stalks densely velvety haired. Young leaflets velvety-haired on both sides, but later nearly hairless above. Fruit finely hairy.

**Manna or Flowering Ash**
*Fraxinus ornus*

 † *

A small round-crowned tree to 20 m with very smooth grey bark. Distinguished from the previous species by the conspicuous conical cluster of creamy-white fragrant flowers which appear at the same time as the leaves at the tips of the branches. It grows in mixed woods, thickets, and rocky places in the Mediterranean region and S.–C. Europe. Buds greyish or brownish, often

a

b

c

d

e

f

bloomed, hairy; twigs olive-green. Leaves with 5–9 ovate to lanceolate, distinctly stalked leaflets, which are irregularly and finely toothed. Leaflets of young trees stalkless, saw-toothed. Flowers with 4 strap-shaped petals 5–6 mm long. Fruit 2–2.5 cm, pointed or notched at the apex. A sugary gum or 'manna' exudes from the branches and is collected and used medicinally. The tree is cultivated for this in S. Italy and Sicily.

## Red Ash
*Fraxinus pennsylvanica*

A N. American tree with brownish-red furrowed bark and distinctly stalked leaflets. Grown for timber and for shelter in C. and S.–E. Europe. Buds small, brown; twigs hairless to densely hairy. Leaflets 5–7, large 8–15 cm long, hairy beneath, variable in width and teething. Fruit not flattened in the lower part.

## Wild Jasmine
*Jasminum fruticans*

A small evergreen or half-evergreen shrub to 3 m, with erect quadrangular, green branches and yellow tubular flowers. It is native in S. Europe in thickets and woodland verges. Leaves mostly trifoliate; leaflets glossy, 1–2 cm. Flowers 1–1.5 cm long, with 5 blunt lobes nearly as long as the yellow tube. Fruit globular, 7–9 mm, black, fleshy.

a    b    c    d    e

## OLIVE FAMILY

**Winter Jasmine** (a)
*Jasminum nudiflorum*

  ‡

**Common White Jasmine** (b)
*Jasminum officinale*

  ‡

The former is widely grown as
an ornamental. A deciduous
shrub with opposite trifoliate
leaves. Flowers yellow, appearing in winter before leaves.
The latter is a climber with
opposite pinnate leaves with
5–7 leaflets. Flowers white,
fragrant, in clusters.

**European Forsythia**
*Forsythia europaea*

A rare deciduous shrub of N.
Albania and S. Yugoslavia, in
hills and on serpentine rocks.
Leaves ovate to lanceolate,
opposite, with toothed or entire
margins. Flowers yellow, appearing before leaves; calyx
and corolla 4-lobed, corolla
tube short, lobes 12 mm (p.
160 (9)). Fruit a pointed capsule,
splitting by 2 valves.

**Common Lilac**
*Syringa vulgaris*

**Hungarian Lilac** (p. 165b)
*Syringa josikaea*

The former is a deciduous shrub
to 3 m, or sometimes a small
tree to 7 m, with ovate leaves
and dense conical clusters of
sweet scented, tubular, lilac,
or rarely white, flowers. Native
in scrub and on rocky slopes
of the central part of the Balkan
peninsula. Widely grown for

a

b

c

d

e

ornament elsewhere. Leaves hairless, 4–8 cm, with a rounded or shallow heart-shaped base, leaf margin toothless. Flowering clusters usually paired, 10–20 cm; flowers tubular, with 4 spreading lobes (p. 160 (7)). Fruit a pointed capsule (p. 160 (3)).
The latter has narrower elliptic leaves with a narrower wedge-shaped base. Inflorescence solitary, leafy at base, with deep violet-mauve, funnel-shaped flowers. Native of mountains of Romania and Ukraine.

a
b
c
d
e

## Privet
*Ligustrum vulgare*

## Oval-Leaved Privet (e)
*Ligustrum ovalifolium*

 ‡

The former is a widely distributed deciduous shrub, usually not more than 3 m high, of W., C., and S. Europe reaching as far north as S. Scandinavia. It is a spreading shrub of wood verges, hedges, and banks, particularly on alkaline soils. Leaves opposite, lanceolate, 3–6 cm, often persisting through the winter. Flowers white, heavily-fragrant, in dense erect terminal clusters; corolla tube about as long as the 4 spreading lobes (p. 160 (1)). Fruit glossy black, 6–8 mm.
The latter is commonly planted for hedges, occasionally in the golden-leaved form. A native of Japan; distinguished from the above by its hairless young twigs, and broader oval, more evergreen leaves. Flower clusters hairless, and corolla tube 2–3 times as long as the lobes.

165

## OLIVE FAMILY

### *Ligustrum lucidum*

  ‡

A small, dense, evergreen tree
to 10 m, or a large shrub, with
hairless twigs with white lenticels. Flowers creamy-white in
comparatively large, lax, branched, conical clusters 12–20
cm. Leaves glossy dark green,
long-pointed, 8–12 cm; young
leaves reddish. Fruit bloomed,
bluish-black. Widely grown as
a roadside tree in S. Europe;
native of China and Japan.

### Olive
### *Olea europaea*

 † *

A familiar and most important
small tree to 15 m, with silvery-
green evergreen foliage, twisted,
often gnarled trunk, and spreading grey branches. Native of
the Mediterranean region and
Portugal, where it is widely
cultivated for its fruit. Cultivated trees have lanceolate
leaves 2–8 cm, pale greyish beneath and covered with small
silvery scales, like the twigs.
Flowers white, in dense axillary
clusters. Fruit ovoid, 1–3.5 cm
long, at first green then usually
becoming black or brownish-
green, or rarely ivory-white.
Wild plants appear very different, often bushy, with spiny,
quadrangular stems and small
oval leaves (c). They are found in
evergreen scrub in dry rocky
places, and in open woods. A
very valuable economic tree.

## *Phillyrea latifolia*

A dense, small-leaved, evergreen shrub or small tree to
15 m, with smooth grey bark.
Found in evergreen woods in
the Mediterranean region and
Portugal. Leaves (2) opposite,
with 7–12 pairs of lateral veins,
either ovate and toothed, or
lanceolate to elliptic with entire
or very finely-toothed margins.
Flowers greenish-white, in
short dense clusters; calyx triangular. Fruit at length bluish-
black, without a point.

## *Phillyrea angustifolia*

A dense, evergreen shrub to
2.5 m with opposite linear to
lanceolate leaves (1), and smooth
grey twigs. Native of evergreen scrub in the Mediterranean region, from Yugoslavia
westwards to Portugal. Leaves
with 4–6 pairs of inconspicuous veins. Calyx with short
rounded lobes. Fruit with a
point.

a

b

*Phillyrea angustifolia* 1

×1

×4

×4 ×1½

*Phillyrea latifolia* 2

c

## DOGBANE FAMILY
### Apocynaceae

### Oleander
*Nerium oleander*

One of the most beautiful and
distinctive shrubs of the Mediterranean region and Portugal.
An evergreen forming con-
spicuous clumps up to 4 m in
dry river beds and on river
banks along the coast, and inland. Often grown for ornament
in the south and sometimes
naturalized. Leaves linear-
lanceolate, 6–12 cm, in whorls of

d

# DOGBANE FAMILY

2, 3, or 4, leathery, grey-green.
Flowers 3–4 cm across, usually
pink but occasionally white,
with 5 large jagged scales in the
throat, in terminal clusters.
Fruit 8–16 cm, reddish-brown;
seeds with a tuft of hairs. The
only large woody European
member of a predominantly
tropical family, the *Apocynaceae*,
which has characteristically a
milky juice in the leaves and
stems, and which in many cases,
as in Oleander, is poisonous.

a

## MILKWEED FAMILY
## Asclepiadaceae

### Silk-Vine
*Periploca graeca*

A deciduous climbing shrub to
12 m, with many-flowered
clusters of distinctive purplish-
brown flowers. Leaves 4–12 cm,
ovate, hairless. Flowers 2 cm
across; corolla with projecting
purple horns. Fruit paired, each
carpel 10–15 cm.
*P. laevigata* has leathery lanceolate
leaves and smaller purple-brown
flowers 1 cm across.

b

*Periploca
laevigata*

× 1½

Silk-Vine

### Cruel Plant
*Araujia sericifera*

A vigorous S. American evergreen climber which is locally
naturalized in S.–W. Europe. It
has stalked, usually few-flowered clusters of scented flowers
1.5–2 cm across, which are
white, striped with pink.
Leaves oblong-ovate, white-
mealy beneath; young stems
downy. Fruit large ovoid, 10 cm,
bloomed; seeds with a tuft of
silky hairs.

c

seed

## Stranglewort
*Cynanchum acutum*

A slender, twining, climber to 3 m with hairless, glaucous arrow-shaped leaves. Flowers pink or white 8–12 mm across, with 5 slender projecting horns (1), sweet scented, in stalked umbels. Fruit (2) of 2 spindle-shaped carpels; seeds with a tuft of hairs. Native of S. Europe in hedges and thickets often near the sea.

a

## WATERLEAF FAMILY
## Hydrophyllaceae

*Wigandia caracasana*

  ‡

A robust, erect, rough-haired shrub to 4 m, with very large oval leaves which are coarsely toothed. Leaf blade 20–45 cm, whitish-hairy beneath. Flowers about 3 cm across, lilac with a pale tube, in large lax clusters with curved branches. Native of C. and S. America; cultivated for ornament and locally natural-ized on walls and rocks in France, Spain, and Italy.

b

ovary and stamen

## VERBENA FAMILY
## Verbenaceae

### Chaste Tree
*Vitex agnus-castus*

A graceful, aromatic, grey-leaved shrub to 4 m, with slender, dense spikes of lilac, pink, or rarely white fragrant flowers. Found by rivers near the sea in S. Europe. Leaves distinctive, with 5–7 narrow lanceolate leaflets which are white-woolly beneath; twigs quadrangular. Flowers two-lipped; stamens projecting.

c

d

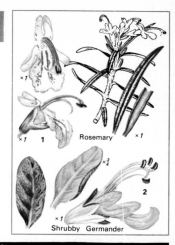

An important family of over 3,000 species with a centre of concentration in the Mediterranean region, where they may be locally dominant. Many are herbaceous plants, many more are small shrubs less than 2 m tall. They characteristically contain aromatic oils and many of our culinary herbs belong to this family. Botanically distinguished by their opposite, usually simple leaves, quadrangular stems, and two-lipped flowers, borne in whorls and often forming spike-like clusters. Calyx tubular, 5-lobed, often two-lipped; stamens usually 4; ovary four-lobed. Fruit of 4 nutlets. Many members of the family are ornamental.

### Rosemary
*Rosmarinus officinalis*

A dense, very aromatic evergreen bush to 2 m or more of dry rocky places in the Mediterranean region and Portugal. Leaves stiff, dark green above, white-woolly beneath with inrolled margins. Flowers blue, rarely pink or white, with 2 long projecting curved stamens and a style (1). An important flavouring herb; often grown for this and for ornament.

### Shrubby Germander
*Teucrium fruticans*

A small evergreen shrub to 2.5 m with white-woolly, quadrangular stems, small shining leaves which are contrastingly white-woolly beneath. Flowers (2) blue or lilac, without an upper lip; stamens 4. Found in the W. Mediterranean region eastwards to Italy and Sicily, in dry open sunny places. Sometimes grown as a hedge plant in the south.

a

b

# NIGHTSHADE FAMILY    Solanaceae

An important family of over 2,000 species, largely of tropical regions and South America. Only about 18 species are natives of Europe and few are woody. Important economically as it contains such valuable food plants as the potato and tomato, and notable drug plants like henbane and belladonna, as well as tobacco. Distinguished by its regular, tubular, 5-lobed flowers (1), with 5 stamens attached to the tube. Ovary usually with 2, many-seeded chambers. Fruit either a berry (2)—usually with a persistent calyx—or a splitting capsule. Many species are ornamental, some have escaped and become locally naturalized; others are weeds of cultivation; many are poisonous.

Duke of Argyll's Tea-Plant

### Duke of Argyll's Tea-Plant
*Lycium barbarum*

One of several similar-looking, spiny shrubs, reaching 2.5 m; this is the most widely naturalized in Europe; native of China. Flowers violet (1) becoming brownish; corolla lobes as long as tube; stamens projecting, their filaments hairy below. *L. europaeum* is native in the Mediterranean region. It has white or pink flowers; hairless filaments and rigid branches with many stout spines.

### *Solanum sodomeum*

A shrubby, much-branched perennial to 3 m, covered with yellow prickles to 1.5 cm long. Leaves deeply lobed, scattered with prickles, and with star-shaped hairs. Flowers violet, 2.5–3 cm across; calyx prickly. Fruit 2–3 cm, a yellow to brown somewhat fleshy, poisonous berry. Native of Africa; naturalized in S. Europe by roadsides and waste places mainly by the sea.

## NIGHTSHADE FAMILY

*Cestrum parqui*

  ‡

A slender-branched, deciduous
shrub to 3 m, with lanceolate
entire leaves, and terminal
clusters of many yellow to
greenish, tubular, night-scented
flowers. Corolla-tube (1) 2–2.5
cm, lobes spreading, acute.
Fruit 7–10 mm, ovoid, blackish;
seeds reddish-brown. Native of
S. America; locally naturalized
in the Mediterranean region.

### Shrub Tobacco
*Nicotiana glauca*

  ‡

A slender, glaucous-leaved
shrub to 6 m or more, distinguished by its drooping clusters
of tubular yellow flowers, each
3–4 cm long. Leaves ovate to
lanceolate, hairless; twigs green.
Fruit an ovoid capsule. Native
of S. America; often grown for
ornament in the Mediterranean
region and frequently naturalized by roadsides, on banks
and walls.

## BUDDLEIA FAMILY
## Buddlejaceae

### Common Buddleia
*Buddleja davidii*

  ‡

A deciduous shrub to 5 m with
lanceolate leaves, quadrangular
woolly-haired twigs, and long,
terminal clusters of lavender-
blue or violet flowers with long
orange corolla-tubes. Flowers
very fragrant and attractive to
butterflies. Leaves dark green
above, white-woolly beneath,
toothed. Commonly naturalized
in urban waste places.

172

## FIGWORT FAMILY
### Scrophulariaceae

**Paulownia, Foxglove-Tree**
*Paulownia tomentosa (imperialis)*

  ‡

A small, round-headed deciduous tree to 12 m, with large
triangular-heart-shaped leaves
and large conical clusters of
violet, trumpet-shaped flowers
each 5–6 cm long. Leaves
opposite, 12–25 cm, but larger
and lobed on vigorous shoots;
twigs woolly-haired. Fruit
woody, 3–4 cm. Native of China;
often planted by roadsides in S.

## BIGNONIA FAMILY
### Bignoniaceae

**Indian Bean-Tree**
*Catalpa bignonioides*

 ‡

A similar-looking tree to the
previous with large triangular
heart-shaped leaves, but
flowers and fruits quite different. Older trees have wide-
spreading branches borne on a
stout pale brown, scaling trunk.
Leaves at first purple on young
trees when emerging, then pale
green, 10–20 cm long, opposite
or often whorled, nearly hairless above. Flower clusters
broadly conical 15–20 cm; flowers tubular, with spreading
lobes, 4–5 cm across. Pods long,
slender, rounded, 20–40 cm,
hanging from the tips of the
branches, and persisting during
the winter. A very distinctive
deciduous tree from N. America;
frequently planted in S. Europe
along boulevards and roadsides,
sometimes escaping in waste
places.

# HONEYSUCKLE FAMILY    Caprifoliaceae

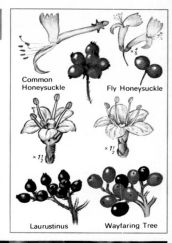

Common Honeysuckle    Fly Honeysuckle

Laurustinus    Wayfaring Tree

A rather small family consisting of elders, viburnums, honey-suckles and snowberries, largely of the northern hemisphere; the majority are woody, some are climbers. 21 species are native to Europe, some of these are small bushes which do not reach 2 m. The family is distinguished by its inferior ovary (the ovary placed below the petals, sepals, and stamens), with 3–5 carpels. Leaves opposite, usually simple. Calyx and corolla 4–5-lobed; stamens 5, attached to the corolla tube. Fruit usually a berry or drupe. A family of no economic importance; a considerable number are grown as ornamentals.

## Elder
### *Sambucus nigra*

  † *

A well-known, large much-branched shrub or small tree to 10 m, with compound leaves, flat-topped clusters of creamy-white strong-smelling flowers, and black shiny fruits. Leaves strong-smelling when crushed; leaflets 5–7, oval to lanceolate, sharply toothed; twigs grey, smooth, with lenticels, and with white pith (1). Flowers about 5 mm across, numerous in large five-rayed clusters 10–20 cm across. Fruit often in hanging clusters, fleshy, 6–8 mm, usually black, but sometimes green. A plant of damp woods, hedges, and waste places throughout Europe, often cultivated in the south.

a

b

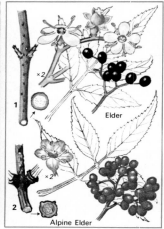

Elder

Alpine Elder

## Alpine or Red-Berried Elder
*Sambucus racemosa*

A shrub to 4 m, like the previous with compound leaves, but flowers greenish-yellow in dense rounded clusters, and fruit scarlet. Twigs with cinnamon-coloured pith (p. 174 (2)). Found in shady woods in the mountains of C. Europe from Spain to Bulgaria; naturalized further north.

## Guelder Rose
*Viburnum opulus*

A spreading deciduous shrub to 4 m, with distinctive flat-topped clusters of white flowers, with the outer ring of much larger flowers (1) surrounding the central mass of smaller flowers. The clusters are 5–10 cm across; the outer flowers to 2 cm across, sterile, the inner fertile, about 8 mm. Leaves usually 3-lobed, the lobes acute, coarsely and irregularly toothed, finely hairy beneath; with a pair of glands at the base of the blade. Leaves colouring scarlet in autumn. Twigs smooth, angled (2). Fruit 8 mm, nearly globular, glistening red and often persisting after the leaves fall. It is widely distributed in Europe, except in the outer fringes of the continent; and is found in damp woods, thickets, and hedges. A form with only large sterile flowers in a globular cluster is often cultivated for ornament.

a

b

c

d

# HONEYSUCKLE FAMILY

## Wayfaring Tree
*Viburnum lantana*

A well-known and distinctive deciduous shrub to 6 m, with grey-felted twigs, heart-shaped, crinkled leaves which are white-woolly beneath, and creamy-white flowers in dense flat-topped clusters. Flowers all fertile and the same size; clusters 6–10 cm across. Leaves 5–12 cm, finely toothed, with short woolly-haired leaf stalks. Buds without scales (1).
Fruit in flat-topped or domed clusters, first green then red and finally black, often ripening unevenly. It is found in wood verges, thickets, hedges, and rocky places throughout most of C. and S. Europe, particularly on calcareous soils.

## Laurustinus
*Viburnum tinus*

A dense, dark, much branched, evergreen shrub to 4 m of the Mediterranean region and Portugal, which is found in woods, evergreen thickets, and stony places, in the hills and down to the coast. Often grown for ornament, and shelter, particularly in the west, where it often flowers throughout the winter. Leaves leathery dark glossy-green, narrowly oval blunt or acute, with smooth

margins, and tufts of hairs in the vein-axils beneath. Twigs smooth or somewhat hairy. Flowers white or pink flushed outside, in small, terminal, flat-topped clusters 5–10 cm across. Fruits metallic blue, in clusters, often hidden amongst the leaves.

a

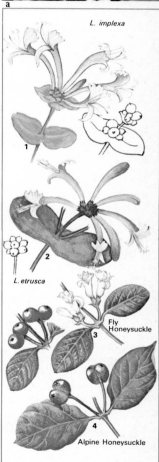

**Key to HONEYSUCKLES** (*Lonicera*)

1 Woody climbers.

  2 Flowers in axillary pairs (3).       **Japanese** (p180), *biflora*

  2 Flowers in heads, or whorls (1) (2).

    3 Leaves directly below inflorescence not fused.     **Common** (p178)

    3 Leaves directly below inflorescence fused round stem (1) (2).

      4 Flower clusters stalked (2).     *etrusca* (p179)

      4 Flower clusters stalkless (1).   **Perfoliate** (p178), *implexa* (p179), *splendida*

1 Erect shrubs.

  5 Twigs and leaves hairless or nearly so.     **Alpine** (p179), *tatarica* (p180)

  5 Twigs, and leaves finely hairy at least on the lower surface.   *arborea, nummulariifolia,* **Fly** (p179)

L. implexa

1

2

L. etrusca

Fly
Honeysuckle

3

4

Alpine Honeysuckle

Local species, growing to over 2 m are: the climbers *L. splendida* from mountains of S. Spain and *L. biflora* from S.–E. Spain, and the shrubs *L. arborea* from the Sierra Nevada, S. Spain and *L. nummulariifolia* from S. Greece and Crete.

## HONEYSUCKLE FAMILY

### Common Honeysuckle
*Lonicera periclymenum*

The most widely dispersed and robust of the European climbing honeysuckles; easily distinguished by the uppermost leaves immediately below the flower clusters (1), which are free like the lower leaves and never fused round the stem. Leaves. oblong to elliptic, blunt or acute, glaucous-green beneath. Flower clusters stalked, in a terminal head, usually glandular-hairy. Flowers very sweet-scented, long-tubed, two-lipped with projecting stamens and style, creamy-white, often pink-flushed. Fruit red, in a stalked cluster. A deciduous climber to 6 m, of W.–C. and S. Europe extending as far north as S. Sweden. One of 3 important forest lianas of Europe, the others being Ivy and Traveller's Joy or Clematis. Often a pest of forestry plantations, damaging young trees.

### Perfoliate Honeysuckle
*Lonicera caprifolium*

Similar in appearance to the preceding species, but easily distinguished by the upper leaves which are fused round the stem i.e. *perfoliate*. Flower clusters stalkless, closely surrounded by a cup-shaped involucre of paired leaves. A less robust and more glaucous climber of bushy places of E.–C. and S. Europe; widely naturalized elsewhere.

a

b

c

178

*Lonicera etrusca* (a)
*Lonicera implexa* (b)

The former (p. 177 (2)) has deciduous or semi-evergreen leaves and stalked clusters of flowers. Uppermost pair of leaves fused.
The latter (p. 177 (1)) has evergreen, bloomed, leathery leaves and stalkless flower clusters surrounded by the cup-like paired leaves. Both are slender climbers in bushy places in the Mediterranean region and Portugal.

**Fly Honeysuckle**
*Lonicera xylosteum*

An erect, branched, deciduous shrub to 3 m, with ovate leaves, and stalked axillary pairs of small yellowish-white flowers (p. 177 (3)). Found in woods and thickets throughout most of Europe, except in the north and south perimeters of the continent. Fruit of paired, unfused scarlet berries.

**Alpine Honeysuckle**
*Lonicera alpigena*

A leafy deciduous shrub to 3 m, of woods, thickets and rocks, usually in limestone mountains, of S. and S.–C. Europe. Flowers two-lipped, yellow to reddish, 12 mm, long-stalked, paired. Leaves 4–11 cm, more or less elliptic, pointed, shining above, hairy beneath, ciliate. Fruit scarlet, berries paired and more or less fused (p. 177 (4)).

# HONEYSUCKLE FAMILY

**Japanese Honeysuckle** (a)
*Lonicera japonica*

  ‡

*Lonicera tatarica* (b)

  ‡

The former is a vigorous climbing shrub with pale semi-evergreen leaves, and paired short-
stalked white flowers, yellowing
with age. Fruit black.
The latter is a hairless non-
climbing shrub to 3 m, with white
to red, sweet-scented flowers,
1.5–2 cm. Fruit red, orange, or
yellow. Both are native of Asia.

**Snowberry**
*Symphoricarpos albus (rivularis)*

   ‡

A slender suckering shrub often
forming thickets, to 3 m, readily
distinguished by its snow-
white, spongy, globular fruits.
Leaves variable, oval entire, or
lobed on sucker shoots. Flowers
pink 5–6 mm, bell-shaped, in
small axillary clusters. Native
of N. America; widely naturalized on banks, hedges, and
rocky places in Europe.

## LILY FAMILY
### Liliaceae

*Smilax aspera*

An evergreen climber with
tendrils, with hooks on stems
and leaves. Flowers fragrant, in
terminal or axillary clusters,
one-sexed. Fruit red. Widespread in the Mediterranean
region and Portugal, in evergreen thickets, and hedges.
*S. excelsa* has leaves with 3
veins, no hooks, and often
spineless stems. Umbels simple.
S.–E. Europe.

a

b

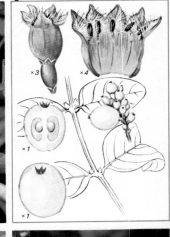

c

d

e

**Century Plant**
*Agave americana*
**Spanish Bayonet** (c)
*Yucca aloifolia*

The former, like the palms, is
often a landmark in the Mediterranean landscape, yet it was
introduced and is a native of
Mexico. The enormous rosettes
of leaves may measure 4 m
across and the flowering spike,
produced once from each rosette
after about 10 years may reach
10 m. Spreading by suckers and
often forming huge impenetrable
clumps. Leaves up to 2 m,
with very sharp tip and spiny
margins, triangular in section.
Flowers yellowish, tubular;
stamens projecting.
The latter is one of several
tree-like Yucca species grown
for ornament and occasionally
naturalized in the Mediterranean region. Leaves glaucous,
stiff, very sharply pointed, 0.5–
1 m long. Flowers in branched
clusters, white tipped with
purple. Fruit edible, like small
bananas, black-purple when ripe.

**Cabbage Tree** (d)
*Cordyline australis*
*Dracaena* species (e)

The former, native of New
Zealand, has hard, pointed
leaves 30–90 cm long. Flowers
creamy, fragrant, about 1.5 cm
across, in clusters with 3 large
bracts at base. Fruit a berry.
*Dracaena* species are like the
former in general appearance
but cells of ovary one-seeded
and inflorescence without
bracts at base. Flowers whitish,
larger.

181

## GRASS FAMILY
### Gramineae

**Giant Reed, Cane**
*Arundo donax*

The largest native European
grass which may reach 5 m and
is bamboo-like. It grows in
ditches and by watersides in
the Mediterranean region and
Portugal. Distinguished from
bamboos by the single leaf arising from each node and clasping the stem. Flower clusters
terminal, plume-like, 40–70 cm
long becoming silvery-brown.

**Metake**
*Arundinaria japonica*

A fast-suckering, Japanese
bamboo, often planted for ornament and sometimes escaping
and persisting for years. It
usually forms dense thickets
3–6 m high in damp places.
Stems round in section, green;
sheaths brown, persistent.
Leaves 2–3 cm broad, long-
pointed, minutely toothed on
margin. Branches usually
arising singly from some of the
upper stem nodes.

**Black Bamboo** (d)
*Phyllostachys nigra*
*Phyllostachys viridi-glaucescens* (e)

A difficult group to identify,
differing from the preceding by
their flattened or grooved canes
with 2–3 branches arising from
each upper stem node. The
former has canes becoming dark
brown to black; the latter has
green then yellowish-green canes
and leaf sheaths with bristles.
Both grow to 5 m or more.

# PALM FAMILY
## Palmaceae

### Date Palm
*Phoenix dactylifera*

A native palm of the humid parts of the Middle East; sometimes grown for ornament in the Mediterranean region. Trunk tall, slender, up to 20 m. Leaves very large, stiff, distinctly grey-green, with numerous pairs of rigid leaflets, somewhat glaucous beneath. Flower clusters large. The well-known edible fruit is reddish-brown.

### Canary Palm
*Phoenix canariensis*

An ornamental palm, native of the Canary Islands, frequently planted as a boulevard tree in the Mediterranean region and sometimes naturalized. It is like the previous species in general appearance but has a shorter stouter trunk 6–8 m and glossy green leaves with less rigid leaflets, which are green beneath. Fruit small, about 1.5 cm, dry, inedible.

### Cretan Palm
*Phoenix theophrasti*

### Coquito Palm of Chile (p. 184b)
*Jubea spectabilis*

The former is a very rare palm, restricted to the eastern part of Crete and found only there. Though its presence has been known since classical times it has only recently been recognized as a distinct species, closely related to the Date

a

b

c

d

e

# PALM FAMILY

Palm. It differs from it in its fruits which are small, 1.5 by 1 cm, dry and inedible. The trunk may reach 10 m. Leaves 3–5 m long, the lower leaflets slender spine-tipped, the upper flattened, grey-green. Flower clusters (a) short-stalked.

The latter is a majestic 'feather' palm which is sometimes planted in boulevards and parks in the Mediterranean region. Its stout, smooth, elephant-grey trunks are unmistakable.

## Dwarf Fan-Palm
*Chamaerops humilis*

This and the Cretan Palm are the only native palms of Europe. It is found along the Mediterranean coast in dry sandy, rocky places, from Italy and Sicily westward, excluding France.

It is a fan-palm, with slender, spiny leaf stalks and a rounded blade cut, like a fan, to one third or more into 12–15 stiff pointed segments. Wild plants are usually stemless, freely suckering and often form clumps (d). In cultivation (c) it may produce a stout fibre-covered trunk several metres high. Flowers yellow, in dense clusters, at first covered by a large reddish sheath. Fruits inedible, about 2 cm.

a

b

c

d

e

## Chusan Palm
*Trachycarpus excelsus*

  ‡

A tall fan-palm often grown as an ornamental in the Mediterranean region. Native of China and Japan. It has a stout, shaggy, fibrous trunk to 9 m. Leaves with rounded blades divided into numerous stiff segments; leaf stalk stoutly toothed. Flowers small, yellow, in branched, down-curved clusters; sheaths many and prominent. Fruit small, globular, blue-black.

## *Washingtonia filifera*

   ‡

A tall fan-palm of California, to 15 m; sometimes planted for ornament along boulevards in the Mediterranean region. Blades of leaves 1–1.5 m across, with numerous segments with copious long pale fibres; the crown sometimes appearing covered by a wig. Leaf stalks with stout yellow spines. Trunk becoming smooth and ringed. Flowers white in long-stalked clusters longer than the leaves.

## BANANA FAMILY
### Musaceae

**Plantain, Banana**
*Musa* species

A tall fan-palm of ‡

Quite unmistakable with their enormous leaves which soon become torn and tattered. Natives of the tropics; cultivated in warmer Mediterranean regions. Flowers in a pendulous spike with broad reddish-purple bracts. Fruits edible. Really huge herbaceous plants, but too conspicuous to be omitted.

a b c d e f

# Barks

1  Silver Fir
2  Norway Spruce
3  European Larch
4  Bosnian Pine
5  Stone Pine, Umbrella Pine
6  Maritime Pine
7  Scots Pine
8  Black Pine

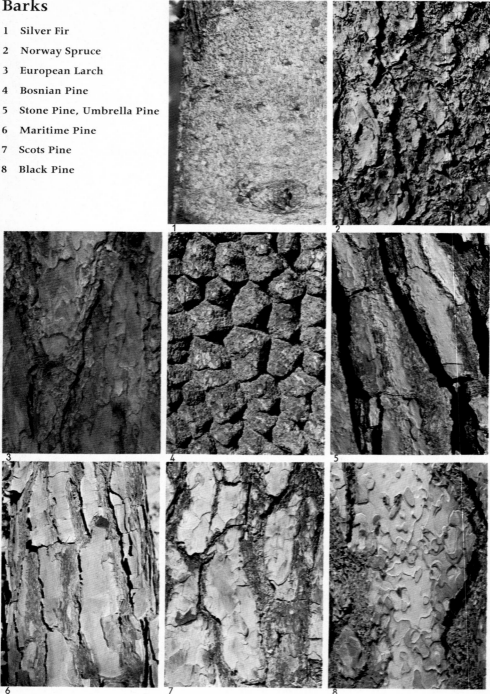

1   Stinking Juniper

2   Yew

3   Crack Willow

4   Sallow

5   White Poplar

6   Aspen

7   Black Italian Poplar

8   Common Walnut

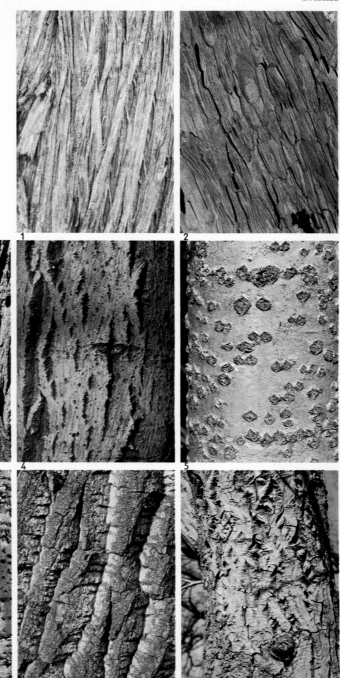

BARKS

1 Silver Birch

2 Common Alder

3 Green Alder

4 Hornbeam

5 Hop-Hornbeam

6 Hazel

7 Beech

8 Sweet Chestnut

1 Holm Oak

2 Cork Oak

3 Kermes Oak

4 Turkey Oak

5 Durmast Oak

6 White Oak

7 English Elm

8 Smooth-Leaved Elm

## BARKS

1 Fig

2 Laurel, Sweet Bay

3 London Plane

4 Oriental Plane

5 Common Pear

6 Apple

7 Service Tree

8 Common Whitebeam

1 Blackthorn, Sloe

2 Wild Cherry, Gean

3 False Acacia

4 Norway Maple

5 Field Maple

6 Sycamore

7 Horse-Chestnut

8 Holly

BARKS

1 Spindle-Tree

2 Broad-Leaved Lime

3 European or Common Lime

4 Greek Strawberry Tree

5 Common Ash

6 Manna Ash

7 Olive

8 Elder

# Uses to man of selected trees and bushes

| | TIMBER | FOOD, MEDICINES, DYES, ETC. | LANDSCAPE AND ENVIRONMENT |
|---|---|---|---|
| **Alder, Common** | Wood soft, durable under water, but not when dry. Used for piles, barrels, clogs; easily turned for toys, broomheads, hat-blocks, and other small articles. Charcoal used for gun-powder making in the past. | The bark is astringent; decoction used for sore throats as a gargle. Important as a dye plant; still used to give browns, blacks, reds, green and yellow with different mordants. Bark was used for tanning leather and fishermen's nets. | Requires water near its roots, often planted to support river banks and lakesides. Can be periodically coppiced, and several stout trunks grow from each stool. Withstands polluted atmospheres; used for wind-breaks and hedging. Roots have nitrogen-fixing nodules. |
| **Almond** | Wood hard, reddish; used for veneers. | Seeds edible when ripe, an important article of commerce; used in cooking and for flavouring. Oil of Bitter Almonds, from which poisonous Prussic acid has been removed, used for flavouring. Sweet oil of almonds is rich in vitamin E, used in toilet creams, and medicinally in the past. | An attractive small tree particularly when flowering early in the year before most other trees. Cultivated in orchards in the south of Europe. |
| **Apples** | Wood brown or reddish, compact and homogeneous but apt to warp and split when drying. Used by turners, cabinet makers, sculptors, and for engraving. Used for making mallet heads and golf clubs. A good fuel wood. | Fruit much in demand fresh for dessert, cooking, jams, marma-lades, jellies etc; it can be dried or canned. Apples make a non-alcoholic drink; fermented they make cider. Fruit rich in vitamin C and pectin, and with general therapeutic properties— 'an apple a day keeps the doctor away!' | Planted in most of Europe except the northern and southern fringes for its fruit. |
| **Ashes** | Wood pale, greyish-white, very strong, tough, and pliant. It cleaves well and does not splinter; it is easily 'bent' when steamed. A valuable timber used for all kinds of tool-handles, sports-equipment, hoops, walk-ing-sticks, furniture, ladder-poles, carts, wheels, etc. Not durable when wet. An excellent fuel wood; makes good charcoal. | Leaves used for cattle fodder in Scandinavia. Bark used for tanning nets. Bark once used to alleviate the symptoms of inter-mittent fevers, agues, etc. Leaves purgative, diuretic; used in arithritic and rheumatic complaints. Manna Ash branches when incised yield a sweet sap, which hardens to the gum 'manna'. Used in pharmacy as a mild laxative for children and during pregnancy. | A handsome quick growing tree, casting little shade and prefering calcareous soils. Withstands coastal winds, and some atmospheric pollution. Should not be planted near buildings as roots can disturb foundations. Often coppiced. Manna Ash an attractive small tree, with heavy-scented flowers, smooth bark: it with-stands some pollution. |
| **Aspen** | Wood light, porous, and easy to split but does not splinter. It stands up to hard wear; used for cart-bottoms, trucks, also for light packing cases and chip boxes. Used for interior work in furniture, and particularly for matches as it does not burn too quickly. Pulp makes a high quality paper. | Bark was once used for tanning; and the twigs for basketry. | An attractive tree with trembling leaves and good autumn colouring. Tolerant to coastal winds and atmospheric pollution. Slower growing than most poplars; it suckers freely. Rich in insect life. |

# USES TO MAN

| | TIMBER | FOOD, MEDICINES, DYES, ETC. | LANDSCAPE AND ENVIRONMENT |
|---|---|---|---|
| **Beech** | Wood fine-grained, smooth, free from knots, and is easily cleaved. Used for furniture, coach-building, tool and brush-handles, wood paving, sabots, and for many domestic turned articles, such as chair legs. Good for fuel and charcoal. Can be bent but less successfully than ash; used for plywood. | Beech seed or 'mast' contains a useful edible oil, which has been used for lighting, cattle cake, feeding hogs and poultry. In Britain good 'mast' years occur every 5–10 years. | A good tree for shelter belts mixed with conifers; excellent hedging plant. Forms fine specimen trees, giving superb autumn colouring. Gives heavy shade and leaf litter; unable to stand polluted atmospheres. Favours calcareous soils or deep sandy loams. |
| **Birch** | Wood hard and strong, but small and not very durable, particularly outdoors. Used mostly in Scandinavia for plywood, furniture, veneers, skis, flooring; also for many small turned articles. Twigs used for brooms and brushes; the bark for roofing, boxes, plates, and for tanning. Good fuel wood. | The sap is sugary, it is fermented for alcoholic drinks, used as a sweetening agent, and as a shampoo. Young leaves rich in saponins and used medicinally. Bark is rich in tannins; it yields Birch tar oil used in the preparation of Russian leather, also as an insect repellent. | Quick growing, short-lived, light demanding; will grow well on light dry soils; shallow-rooting and casts little shade. Can be coppiced; quickly sprouts from the base after fires. Clumps of trees can be very picturesque. High wildlife value. |
| **Blackthorn, Sloe** | Wood hard, tough, strongly veined and takes a good polish; sometimes used for marquetry. Stems used for walking sticks, and handles. | Fruits very astringent only edible when fully ripe, used for jam making and flavouring gin, and can be fermented. Leaves and bark astringent; the former have been used as a substitute for tea. | Used for hedging, usually mixed with hawthorn, which keeps farm stock within the field boundary. High wild-life value; vandal proof. |
| **Box** | Wood hard, heavy, very close- and even-grained. Highly valued for engraving, carving, and printing blocks, inlay and marquetry; also used for small mathematical instruments, spindles, rollers, small tool handles. | Leaves and seeds strongly purgative. Herbally used as a blood purifier. Homoeopathically used against rheumatism, also in veterinary work to improve general condition. | Slow growing, hardy, evergreen, good for screening or as a decorative hedge. Withstands clipping well, and as with yew is excellent for topiary. Withstands shade and some pollution; useful game cover. |
| **Buckthorns** | Buckthorn has a hard, dense, and reddish-brown wood; it has no special uses. Alder Buckthorn produces a high quality charcoal, which was used until recently for the manufacture of gunpowder. | Fruits of Buckthorn purgative; formerly used medicinally. Syrup from fruits used in veterinary work. The fruits give a sap-green dye, and a pigment of similar colour. Fruit and bark of Alder Buckthorn when fresh are emetic; the dried bark is a purgative and used medicinally. The fruit gives a bluish-grey dye, the bark a yellow or brown with different mordants. Persian berries, known in the dyeing trade, are the fruits of other buckthorn species; they give a good green dye. | Buckthorn prefers alkaline soils. Alder Buckthorn grows in the wild in poor wet acid soils. |

| | TIMBER | FOOD, MEDICINES, DYES, ETC. | LANDSCAPE AND ENVIRONMENT |
|---|---|---|---|
| **Carob, Locust Tree** | Wood reddish-wine-coloured when matured. Used in cabinet-making, for marquetry, and by wheelwrights. It deteriorates with humidity. | Seeds contain 40% sucrose, 17% reducing sugar, and about 10% protein; a valuable food for cattle, horses and pigs, and also for humans in times of shortage. Locust Bean gum is used in paper-making, as a food-stabilizer, in tobacco-curing and for fermented beverages. Bark and leaves used for tanning. | A valuable shade tree in low rainfall areas of the Mediterranean region; often planted by roadsides. Grows in dry rocky soils. |
| **Cherry** | Wood a warm yellow-green to light reddish-brown. Stable when seasoned and highly prized for cabinet-making; also used for turnery, particularly for bored and pierced work, like pipes and musical instruments. | The familiar edible fruit is consumed fresh, in conserves, or as alcoholic beverages and liqueurs, such as maraschino, ratafia, kirschwasser, cherry brandy. The bark gives a yellow dye. Fruit stalks used to make a tonic. Cherry syrup—from Black Cherry—used for coughs. | Ornamental tree, particularly during spring flowering and autumn colouring. There are many ornamental species and varieties widely planted in urban areas; many withstand pollution. Good honey flowers. |
| **Chestnut, Horse-** | Wood soft, fine-grained, does not crack or split; used for joinery, cabinet-making, turnery, boxes, etc. | Seeds not edible; used as cattle and horse fodder in eastern Europe. Seeds contain saponins. Aescin is extracted commercially and used medicinally for re-absorbing intercellular water, as in oedema and varicose veins. Bark yields a good black dye for silks and cottons. | Quick growing; casting heavy shade and very ornamental, particularly when in flower and with rich autumn colouring. Able to withstand pollution well. Good for single planting. Favours a moist but well-drained soil. |
| **Chestnut, Sweet** | Timber, though strong and durable, not valuable because it splits and has 'shakes'. Good for outdoor work, for posts, stakes, fencing. Used for boarding, coffins, rough furniture, sleepers, wine barrels. Often coppiced for small poles and cleft-pale fencing, walking sticks, etc. | Nuts are an important article of food in central and southern Europe, used for flour, bread making, and in cookery. Also used for fattening stock. Leaf infusions used in respiratory infections, a popular remedy for whooping cough. Much used homoeopathically. | A fast growing monumental tree with magnificent bark which twists with age, and with good autumn colouring. It favours dry sandy soils. |
| **Cypress, Italian or Funeral** | Wood very hard, durable and aromatic and very resistant to decay. It is much sought after for furniture and carving. Also used for stakes and vine props. | Crushed leaves and seeds have been used medicinally. | A very ornamental tree, particularly the slender columnar forms, often the only vertical feature in Mediterranean landscapes. Commonly planted in graveyards, by boundary walls and near habitation. |
| **Elder** | Wood yellowish-white, hard, strong, useful for small articles like combs, toys, and a substitute for boxwood in very small sections. Elder pith used for cutting botanical sections, and removing oil and dirt from | Flowers and fruit used for fermented beverages; elderberry wine an old cure for coughs. Fruit rich in vitamin C. Many parts of the shrub used in the past in cottage remedies. Bark is purgative. Bark gives a | Shrub colonizes village and town rubbish dumps. |

| | TIMBER | FOOD, MEDICINES, DYES, ETC. | LANDSCAPE AND ENVIRONMENT |
|---|---|---|---|
| | delicate instruments like watches. | black dye, the leaves a green, fruit a blue, lilac, or violet dye with different mordants. | |
| Elms | Wood tough, heavy, and impossible to split, it warps and is very hard to season. Very durable when permanently waterlogged, consequently used for boat-building, bridges, piles, groins, weather-boarding, coffins, and general rough carpentry; also for turnery. It can withstand great strains and is used for capstans, pulleys, water-pumps, etc. | Used medicinally in the past as a cure for ringworm. Inner bark contains mucilage and tannins. Used in homoeopathy. | Smooth-Leaved Elm and pyramidal forms such as Jersey and Cornish Elms are used for avenues and street planting, being resistant to pollution and salt-laden winds. Wych Elm good for exposed situations and atmospheric pollution. English Elm is unsuitable. Dutch Elm disease now seriously threatens all elms; Huntingdon and 'Groenweld' Elms are safest to plant. |
| Fig | Wood tough but porous and easy to bend but of little value. | Dried fruit are a staple winter food in some Mediterranean regions. Figs used medicinally as a poultice for external wounds, boils, also internally as a laxative. The fresh juice from the leaves is used to cure warts. | Often grown for shade and shelter in courtyards, by walls and wells in the south. |
| Fir, Silver | Timber white or yellowish, soft, light and not very strong; it is straight-grained, splits well and works easily. Used largely for indoor work, planks, joinery, sounding boards for musical instruments, carving, boxes and paper pulp. It does not last outdoors. | Bark blisters yield 'Strasbourg Turpentine' which is used in paints and varnishes. Oil of turpentine is distilled from the leaves and wood, used medicinally and in veterinary practice for sprains and bruises. | An important central European tree forming often pure forests in the mountains. |
| Grape Vine | Wood fine-grained and very resistant. Used for posts and stakes. | Fruit eaten fresh, or dried as raisins, sultanas, or currants. Widely grown for its wine and brandy production, and for vinegar. A drying oil is obtained from the crushed seeds. Vine leaves are used in cooking. The tendrils and sap are used in country remedies. | Often planted for shade and shelter in gardens and courtyards in the south. Usually grown in vineyards, either in flat ground or terraced slopes. |
| Hawthorns | The wood is hard, fine-grained, and takes a fine polish. It is small and used for small articles such as walking sticks, rake teeth, tool handles. A hot burning fuel; good for charcoal. | Fruits and flowers of many species make good fermented beverages. Azarole is cultivated for its edible fruits used in conserves and jellies in southern Europe. Flowers used in a tincture as a cardiac tonic. | Common Hawthorn valuable for hedging, windbreaks, and field boundaries, being impenetrable to livestock. Withstands regular cutting and laying, and tolerates polluted atmospheres and salt winds. High wild-life value; somewhat vandal proof. |
| Hazel | Wood white or reddish, soft and easily split, but tough and | Nuts edible, and dry well for winter use. | Used for hedging; can withstand regular cutting. |

| | TIMBER | FOOD, MEDICINES, DYES, ETC. | LANDSCAPE AND ENVIRONMENT |
|---|---|---|---|
| | flexible. Used for hurdles, pea-sticks, hedge stakes, salmon traps, and in the past for thatching spars, wattle and daub building, and peg-making. Often regularly coppiced for small rods. | | |
| Holly | Wood whitish, hard, heavy and fine-grained; it is much in demand for cabinet-making, turnery, and marquetry. To retain whitish colour cut in winter and convert before hot weather. Also used for printing blocks, mathematical instruments, wood engraving, and whip handles. | The berries are poisonous. Young leaves formerly used for fevers and rheumatism. The bark can be made to yield bird-lime. The foliage and fruit are used as Christmas decorations. | Valuable as a hedge and screen tree; withstands clipping and pollarding. Tolerates pollution, so good for industrial, coastal, and urban plantings, and in parks. There are many ornamental cultivated forms. |
| Hornbeam | Wood very hard and tough but not easy to work. It can resist heavy blows and is used for balls, mallets, brush-backs, pulleys, wooden rollers, and skittles. It is often coppiced and cut every 15–35 years. | Good heating fuel. | Excellent for clipped hedges. Slow growing; with good autumn colouring. Withstands some pollution, and shade, and is wind firm. |
| Juniper | Wood durable and with a delicate and lasting fragrance. It is used for making small objects. | Fruit used for flavouring gin, and as a condiment. Oil extracted from the fruits. Whole plant used as a diuretic; also used homoeopathically. Savin yields a poisonous oil; Prickly Juniper yields 'Oil of Cade', both of which are used medicinally and in veterinary work. | Usually small ornamental trees with neat conical forms, and dense foliage. Often planted to to contrast with the deciduous foliage of surrounding trees and shrubs. |
| Larch | Wood reddish-brown, hard, coarse-grained, and durable in contact with the ground. Used for telegraph poles, stakes, railway sleepers, pit-props, also for boat-building, gates and fencing. In central Europe it is split to make pails and churns and other farm utensils. A good heating wood; good for charcoal. | Bark rich in tannins, used in tanning and dyeing. 'Venice Turpentine', used in veterinary work, is obtained by tapping. A sweet gum, obtained from the leaves in summer, formerly used medicinally. Ethyl alcohol is distilled from the wood. | Quick growing; grows well in mountainous areas; requires well drained soils. Its conical form contrasts well with other deciduous trees. Good spring and autumn colouring. In forest plantations often used as nurses for slower growing trees. |
| Laurel, Sweet Bay | Wood sweet scented; used for marquetry. | Leaves used for cooking and flavouring. Yields 'Oil of Bay' which was formerly used medicinally in rheumatism. Used in veterinary work, and sometimes in perfumery. Leaves used as a symbol of victory. | A dense evergreen tree with a distinctive conical form. It grows well by the sea, and can withstand clipping, but it is susceptible to early frosts. |

# USES TO MAN

| | TIMBER | FOOD, MEDICINES, DYES, ETC. | LANDSCAPE AND ENVIRONMENT |
|---|---|---|---|
| **Limes** | Wood white, rather soft, but of even consistency. Excellent for carving, turnery and also for sounding boards for pianos and organs. Used for cutting blocks, hat-blocks, and wood pulp. Fibres of inner bark used for matting, nets, ropes in the past. | Dried flowers make a tea-like infusion which promotes sweating, is antispasmodic and used for catarrh. Honey from lime flowers is distinctive and one of the best flavoured. | Common Lime was widely planted as an ornamental or shade tree in avenues and parks, but it becomes disfigured with honeydew and sucker growth in summer. Broad-Leaved Lime suckers less; Caucasian Lime is the cleanest species, and withstands pollution. Small-Leaved Lime, good in urban situations; transplants at large size. |
| **Maple** | Wood of Field Maple at first white then brownish, compact, firm and with a fine grain. Mostly occurs as small timber which is used for turning and for wood carving. Norway Maple wood is very hard and used for joinery, furniture, and turnery. | A sugar has been obtained from the sap in Scandinavia. | Field Maple is a very hardy small tree, sometimes used for hedging. Good autumn colouring, and sometimes grown as an ornamental tree. Norway Maple, much used in parks, urban areas, shelter belts, is smoke resistant. Attractive early flowers; good autumn colouring. |
| **Mastic Tree** | | Stems, when incised, yield a balsamic sap—the mastic of commerce— which is aromatic and astringent. Used as a varnish for pictures, in perfumery, pharmaceuticals, and dentistry; also as a chewing gum and for flavouring. | |
| **Myrtle** | Wood hard, knotty and mottled; it is valued for turnery. | Leaves, flowers and fruits rich in an aromatic oil, 'Eau d' Anges', used in perfumery. Fruits have been used as a condiment and fermented for a beverage. Bark and roots used for tanning the finest Turkish and Russian leather and imparting to it a delicate aroma. | An ornamental aromatic evergreen shrub. Susceptible to frosts and in the north must be planted in sheltered sunny places. |
| **Nettle Tree** | Wood small, hard and straight; it has been used for walking sticks, tool handles, ramrods, and for joinery. Makes good charcoal. | Fruits edible, and the seeds contain a sweet oil. The bark gives a yellow dye. | Often planted for shade and ornament along roads in southern Europe. |
| **Oak, Common or Pedunculate** | A heavy brown wood, hard, strong, tough, and resistant to rotting. Used for many purposes: building, ship-building, railway carriages, furniture, barrel-making, chests, etc. Used for panelling and stakes. Excellent firewood. | Bark rich in tannins, widely used in tanneries, also gives black, brown or yellow dyes. Fruit produces a non-drying oil; used for feeding pigs. Galls with iron for ink making. Galls also used medicinally for diarrhoea. | Long living, slow growing tree; monumental when grown in isolation and often planted in parks. Tolerant of a wide range of soils. Can be coppiced; care needed with transplanting large trees. Very high wild-life value; the best tree for insects. |

| | TIMBER | FOOD, MEDICINES, DYES, ETC. | LANDSCAPE AND ENVIRONMENT |
|---|---|---|---|
| **Oak, Cork** | Wood heavy, easily warps, and of no value for heavy construction work, but used in joinery. A good fuel wood. | Cork removed every ten or so years, leaving the cambium to form new bark layers. Airtight corks and bungs are cut from sheets of cork parallel to the diameter of the tree. Cork used for many purposes including shoe soles, flooring, floats, life-buoys, and insulating board. | Cork trees are planted in open woods, with either scrub beneath, or the ground below is kept open. |
| **Oak, Holm** | Wood hard and durable, used by wheelwrights, joiners, and for vine props. It makes good charcoal and is valuable for fuel. | Bark very rich in tannins and used for tanning leather and for dyeing. Valonia is the commercial name for the large acorn cups of the Valonia Oak, which are exported from eastern Europe for tanning and dyeing. | A fine evergreen tree which thrives well in the west and is often planted for ornament. Able to withstand sea winds and atmospheric pollution; a useful shelter tree in exposed situations inland. |
| **Oak, Kermes or Holly** | Wood of little value except for fuel and charcoal. | Bark rich in tannins, used for leather tanning and dyeing wools black. The once famous scarlet dyes obtained from small scale insects which feed on the leaves of this tree are now replaced by modern synthetic dyes. | It can grow into a small neat compact evergreen tree if left undisturbed in the south. |
| **Olive** | Wood very hard, takes a fine polish and is strongly grained. It is used for carving, cabinet work, toys, etc.; makes good fuel and charcoal. | The world fruit production is about 1 million tons, and olive orchards can remain productive for several hundred years. The fruit yields a high quality oil, used in cooking, as a lubricant, for lighting and soap making. Oil used medicinally internally as a lubricant and mild laxative, externally in ointments, liniments for the skin and rheumatism. Residue from oil extraction used as cattle food, and fuel. | A very rustic, ornamental tree in the hotter regions of the south; an 'indicator tree' of a Mediterranean climate. Usually planted in orchards, often on terraces; also in gardens for shade and fruit. |
| **Pears** | Wood of old trees hard, compact and takes polish well; valued by turners, cabinet makers and carvers; also used for wood blocks and for printing. Sometimes used to make draughtsmen's instruments. It makes good fuel and charcoal. | Fruit usually edible, either fresh or dried. It makes an alcoholic beverage, 'perry', similar to cider. The bark gives a yellow dye; it contains 'arbutin' which has an anti-bacterial action. Leaf infusions used for renal and urinary infections in southern Europe. | Many cultivated varieties are grown in orchards and gardens throughout most of Europe. |
| **Pine, Aleppo** | Wood used for small timber work, furniture, boat-building in the Mediterranean region. It is coarse-grained, resinous, and relatively poor in quality. Good for fuel. | A resin is obtained from the tree by tapping; it yields good quality oil of turpentine. Resin also used for flavouring; and preserving wine—retsina. Bark used for tanning skins. | A valuable tree on the shallow limestone soils of the drier parts of the Mediterranean region. It withstands coastal exposure well, is drought resistant, checks soil erosion, and acts as a windbreak. |

# USES TO MAN

| | TIMBER | FOOD, MEDICINES, DYES, ETC. | LANDSCAPE AND ENVIRONMENT |
|---|---|---|---|
| **Pine, Arolla** | Wood resinous, pale, straight-grained, smooth, soft, and easily worked. Used locally for cabinet-making, turnery, furniture, shingles, and toy making in central Europe. | The edible seeds are gathered in Switzerland and Russia; they are eaten fresh or used in flavouring and decorating cakes. The husks yield a 'Cedar Oil'. | |
| **Pines, Black (Austrian, Corsican)** | Of the Black Pines the timber of Corsican is best. It is hard, strong, resinous, and used for general construction work in the Mediterranean. | Yields resin and the various products associated with it. | The Austrian Pine is a sombre rather ugly tree, but very resistant to winds and coastal exposure. Used for shelter belts and sand-dune stabilization; tolerant of pollution. The Corsican Pine has a more attractive form but is less tolerant of coastal exposure. |
| **Pine, Maritime** | Wood used for general building purposes, railway sleepers, telegraph poles, pit-props, piles, paving blocks, and paper pulp. Not very durable in soil unless creosoted. | Often tapped for resin, yielding oil of turpentine and other products. Turpentine is used as solvent of paints and varnishes, and for loading paper to take printers ink without smearing. Rosin is used for paints, varnish, linoleum, and soap. Resinous products also produced from distillation of wood. | Valuable tree for stabilizing coastal dunes and sands. Thrives in light well-drained soils. |
| **Pine, Scots** | Timber if clean and free from knots is one of the best soft woods for general construction, boat-building, and joinery. Also used for outdoor work such as sleepers, pit-props, telegraph poles, fencing, heavy boxes, as well as chip-board, hard-boards, paper pulp, cellophane and plastics. | It yields resin from which oil of turpentine is distilled leaving rosin. Also a source of pitch and tar. Resins and oils used as cough cures in the past; pine tar is antiseptic. Pine cones give a reddish-yellow dye. | Good for planting in light acid soils, heaths and moors but it dislikes badly drained soils and coastal exposure. If well grown, a fine hardy ornamental tree with attractive red bark, best planted in small groups. Good wild-life tree. |
| **Pine, Stone or Umbrella** | Wood less resinous than other pines; used for furniture making and local construction. | Seeds edible, much in demand as a food either raw or roasted, and used for flavouring in cooking. | A picturesque, shade-giving, umbrella-shaped tree which withstands coastal exposure well. Often grown in forests near the sea in the Mediterranean region for its seeds. |
| **Planes** | Wood pale, silky textured, with often beautifully marked graining; polishes well. Veneers made from this wood are much in demand by cabinet makers. | | London Plane is a valuable town tree; it stands pollution well, and thrives in restricted places. Can be pollarded or pleached, and throws a rather light shade; it transplants well. Oriental Plane is slower growing, less tolerant of pollution, and is commonly grown as a small town or village shade tree in S. Europe where it may reach very large proportions. |

| | TIMBER | FOOD, MEDICINES, DYES, ETC. | LANDSCAPE AND ENVIRONMENT |
|---|---|---|---|
| Plums | Wood red-veined, hard, close and compact, and takes polish well. Valued by cabinet makers, turners, joiners, and used for block making. | Plums, damsons, greengages, etc. are consumed fresh or dried, and are used for jams, conserves, and alcoholic beverages. Gum extracted from the trunk is used in place of gum arabic and to flavour cider. Seeds yield essence of bitter almonds. The fruit gives a blue dye, and the bark a reddish-brown dye. | Planted in orchards or gardens for its fruit over much of Europe. |
| Pomegranate | | Fruit is eaten fresh, and pulp is used to make cooling drinks and sherberts. Rind and bark rich in tannins, used for tanning Morocco leather. Bark, root and rind of fruit was much valued medicinally in the past, particularly as a vermifuge. From rind and flowers pinkish-red dyes are obtained. | Often grown in gardens in the south both for its fruit and its attractive flowers. Some cultivated varieties have double flowers. A famous plant known to Egyptians and Chinese since the second millennium B.C. |
| Poplars | Wood soft, pale, light and 'woolly'; easily cleaved and used for similar purposes as willow, for veneers, chip-baskets, clogs. Burns slowly, therefore used for matches. | Bark once used for tanning. | Very quick growing; some hybrids grow up to 2 metres a year, consequently useful for screening of factories, railways, etc. Able to withstand pollution and coastal exposure. Favours damp ground, roots spread in search of water. Trees should be planted 30 metres or more away from buildings or drains. |
| Rowan, Mountain Ash | Wood hard and dense, dark-brownish; used for tool handles, farm implements, and for turnery and carving. Twigs sometimes used for basketry. | The fruit can be used to make a jelly and an alcoholic drink. Rich in vitamin C; the 'sugar' is mainly sorbose which can be used in place of cane sugar by diabetics. Fruit used in country remedies to promote urine; the leaves are astringent. Bark was used for tanning. | Small, short-lived ornamental tree, tolerant of most soils and atmospheric pollution. Particularly attractive in spring with masses of white flowers which yield good honey, and in autumn with red fruits and often good autumn colouring, particularly in the north. Gives light shade. Can be planted near buildings. |
| Spindle-Tree | Wood pale, porous yet hard, and splits easily into fine strips, therefore used for making knitting needles, pegs, tooth-picks, manicure sticks, skewers, and spindles. Used in marquetry and small turnery work. Makes excellent artists' charcoal. | The only British woody plant found to have promising insecticidal properties. Fruits acid, poisonous, and purgative. They have been used externally against parasites and mange in animals. The fruits give orange and red dyes. | Grows in the wild on chalk and limestone soils. A host for overwintering Black Aphid. |

201

| | TIMBER | FOOD, MEDICINES, DYES, ETC. | LANDSCAPE AND ENVIRONMENT |
|---|---|---|---|
| Spruce, Norway | The wood splits well, and is light and strong. Used for many purposes such as roofing shingles, barrels, boxes, poles, chip-board, paper pulp, and fuel. Much interior fitting and joinery work is done with this wood; being very resonant, it is used for the bellies of cellos and violins. Easily shredded; fibres woven into mats and screens. | Turpentine is obtained from the bladdery vesicles on the trunk and branches. Also yields Burgundy pitch. The bark used for tanning in Germany today. | Used for the Christmas tree. |
| Strawberry Tree | Wood red-brown, hard; used for decorative carving. Produces good charcoal and good fuel. | Fruit edible, though not usually very palatable. Used to make alcoholic beverages in Spain and Corsica. The bark has been used for tanning leather in Greece. | Sometimes planted for shelter; it withstands coastal exposure well. One of the few ericaceous trees tolerant of calcareous soils. |
| Sycamore | Wood white to yellowish with a silky lustre; clean and compact and has little grain. Used for turnery, carving, furniture making, joinery and violin making; many household and dairy implements such as ladles, spoons, bowls, plates, rollers, etc. are made from it. Much in demand for its smooth beautifully marked veneers. Excellent as firewood. | | A very hardy tree; planted as windbreaks in exposed hill localities. Tolerant of pollution and planted in the past in town parks, avenues, where its coarse dense foliage casts heavy shade. Very poor for wild-life. |
| Terebinth, Turpentine Tree | Wood dark, hard, close-grained, and polishes well; used in cabinet-making and marquetry. | Yields a mild, sweet-tasting gum which solidifies in the air and is used medicinally. An oil is extracted from the fruits. Galls formed on the leaves are used for tanning; they produce a reddish dye. The bark is rich in tannins. | |
| Walnut | Wood homogeneous, strongly-figured, dark-coloured, and much valued by cabinet and furniture makers. Also used by turners, carvers, and for veneers, and for gun-stocks as it withstands shock well. | The seeds are an important article of food, eaten fresh, or used in cooking and for flavouring. Unripe fruits can be pickled. Seeds yield a delicate edible oil, used also by paint-makers and in soap making. Leaves stimulant and astringent, and infusions formerly used for skin diseases. Fruit, husks, and other parts produce a fast brown dye, used also for staining floors. Husks rich in vitamin C. | A handsome, slow-growing tree which favours deep light loams and chalk or limestones. Best planted individually, it takes about 100 years to reach maturity. |

|  | TIMBER | FOOD, MEDICINES, DYES, ETC | LANDSCAPE AND ENVIRONMENT |
|---|---|---|---|
| **Whitebeam** | Wood hard, tough, yellowish; used by carvers and turners, for handles and spoons etc., and also for plywood. | A table jelly, especially for eating with venison, can be prepared from the ripe fruits. | Grows well on light porous loams, particularly on chalk and limestone; withstands pollution and coastal exposure. It is sometimes planted as a street tree—Swedish Whitebeam is also planted. |
| **Willows and Osiers** | Wood light, firm, easily splits but withstands blows and compression. Used for cricket bats, flooring, cart bottoms, artificial limbs, etc. Osiers are the whippy stems cut from stools of certain species which can be bent and woven into baskets, fishing traps, etc. Pollarded willows give periodic crops of small wood used for screens, hurdles, and veneers. Produces high quality charcoal. | Yields the drug salicin, with properties similar to quinine; it is a tonic, but has mainly been used as an anti-malarial, and for rheumatism. Willow roots give bluish-red dyes. Bark used for tanning. | Very valuable for supporting and maintaining river banks, lake verges. Tolerant of polluted atmospheres and coastal winds. Very readily propagated by cuttings stuck in the ground. Fast growing; keep away from drains and foundations of buildings. High wild-life value especially for insects. |
| **Yew** | Wood very hard, elastic, close-grained, dark reddish-brown, and very durable. Used for furniture, flooring, panelling, stakes, barrel-hoops, whip-stocks, mallets, and small tool handles, and for long-bows in the past. Also used for carving and turnery. The wood is very durable outdoors. | Foliage poisonous to animals, particularly when cut and wilted. All parts are poisonous to humans, particularly the seeds, but not the fleshy mucilaginous red covering to the seeds. | An ornamental, dense, dark-foliaged, long-lived, very hardy tree. Withstands polluted atmospheres well; will grow in sun or shade. A very good but slow-growing hedge shrub which can be regularly clipped; it is used for the best topiary work. |

# Index